THE JUST

THE JUST

PAUL RICOEUR

Translated by

DAVID PELLAUER

The University of Chicago Press
Chicago and London

PAUL RICOEUR is John Nuveen Professor Emeritus in the Divinity School, the Department of Philosophy, and the Committee on Social Thought at the University of Chicago. Among his many books are *Oneself as Another* (1992), the three-volume *Time and Narrative* (1984–88), and, most recently, *Thinking Biblically: Exegetical and Hermeneutical Studies* (1998, with André LaCocque), all published by the University of Chicago Press.

The University of Chicago Press, Chicago 60637
The University of Chicago Press, Ltd., London
© 2000 by The University of Chicago
All rights reserved. Published 2000
Printed in the United States of America
09 08 07 06 05 04 03 02 01 00   1 2 3 4 5

B2430
.R553
J8713
2000

ISBN: 0-226-71339-3 (cloth)

Originally published as *Le Juste,* © Éditions Esprit, 1995

Library of Congress Cataloging-in-Publication Data

Ricœur, Paul.
    [Juste. English]
    The just / Paul Ricoeur ; translated by David Pellauer.
      p. cm.
    Includes bibliographical references and index.
    ISBN 0-226-71339-3 (cloth : alk. paper)
    1. Justice (Philosophy) 2. Law—(Philosophy. I. Title.
B2430.R553J8713 2000
174'.2—dc21   99-40311
                                            CIP

Contents

P REFACE

The equitable, while being just, is not the just according to the law, but is rather a corrective to legal justice. The reason for this is that the law is always in a way universal, and there are cases for which it is not possible to offer a general assertion that applies to them with certitude. . . . One sees clearly therefore what the equitable is, that the equitable is just and that it is superior in a certain way to the just.

Aristotle, *Nicomachean Ethics,* Book V, 1137b (J. Tricot translation)

I

The texts brought together in this volume do not properly speaking constitute the chapters of a book. They are lectures given in various places (the details of which are spelled out in the "Sources of Original Publication") under the—beneficial—constraints of programs for which I did not choose the designated topic. Yet these texts do not come down simply to being occasional writings for some particular circumstance. They allowed me, as a philosophy professor, to express one of my oldest preoccupations, having to do with the few cases within our discipline that deal with issues stemming from the juridical arena, compared with the care given to questions having to do with ethics or politics. This neglect of the juridical is all the more surprising in that it is relatively recent. Plato's *Republic* is so closely bound up with the question of justice that tradition has made this idea the subtitle of this well-known dialogue. As for Aristotle, in his ethics he presents a detailed analysis of the virtue of justice. And in the beginning of the modern period, contractual theories of the social bond were worked out in relation to theories of natural law. The philosophies of Hobbes, Machiavelli, and Adam Smith are political theories only to the extent that they propose an explication of the origin and end of law. Leibniz and Kant even composed treatises expressly devoted to the notions of right and law. Nor can we avoid reference to Hegel's *Principles of the Philosophy of Right,* which often served professional philosophers of my generation as the only basis for reflections on the sequence ethics-law-politics. But even there it was the link between ethics and politics that was the principal object of concern, while there was an impasse over the specific status of the juridical.

How are we to account for this general negligence? The shock produced by the outbreaks of violence during our horrifying twentieth century explains in large part this losing sight of the juridical problematic in favor of what we can qualify in general terms as the ethico-political. Yet this neglect undercuts the one discipline as much as the other, inasmuch as the latter culminates in the question of the *legitimacy* of the order by means of which the State makes use of violence, even at the price of that other form of violence from which political power itself stems and whose stigmata it continues to bear. Did not the failure of the Terror during the French Revolution have something to do with the incapacity of the Revolution to stabilize itself through a constitution that would have ensured its perpetuity? Does not the whole of Hegel's political philosophy come down to this question of a constitution? If, nevertheless, we have not given as much attention to this problem of the legitimacy of the constitutional order that defines the State as one based on the rule of law,[1] is it not because, instead of dwelling on the *topos* of the Hege-lian philosophy of right, we have all too willingly allowed our gaze to turn in the direction of the philosophy of history? For Hegel, this follows from his theory of the State once there is no constitutional regime to bring an end to the violent relations among States, which posit themselves on the world scene like great individual violent actors. Once this threshold where the philosophy of history takes over from the philosophy of right has been crossed, it is the drama of war that captures our intellectual energy, at the price of an oft repeated confession of the incomprehensibility in principle of political evil. I am far from deploring, much less reproving, this obstinate return of the eminently historical problem of political evil,

---

1. I have, in fact, taken up some of them in *Lectures I: autour du politique* (Paris: Seuil, 1991).

inasmuch as I myself have contributed to it.[2] So it is with the sense of resisting a line of thought strongly encouraged by the spirit of our times that I have undertaken over the past few years to do justice to the question of right and law, to do justice to justice. My work with the Institut des Hautes Etudes pour la Justice has been particularly influential in that regard. There I encountered the question of the unjust and the just on a level where reflection on the juridical ran little risk of being prematurely taken up into a political philosophy, itself snatched up by a philosophy of history haunted in turn by the pitiless torment arising from and sustained by the aporia of political evil. At the Ecole Nationale de la Magistrature, the training school for public prosecutors and judges, I met the question of the *juridical* in the figure of the *judiciary,* with its written laws, its tribunals, its judges, its ceremonial processes, and, as a capstone to all this, the pronouncement of a sentence where the law is stated in the circumstances of a trial, an eminently singular affair. In this way I was led to believe that the juridical, comprehended through the features of the judiciary, could provide philosophy the occasion to reflect upon the specificity of right and the law, in its proper setting, midway between moral philosophy or ethics (the nuance separating these two not being of importance at this preliminary stage of my investigation) and politics. In order to give a dramatic turn to the opposition I am making here between a political philosophy, where the question of law is covered over by the haunting question of the irrepressible presence of evil in history, and a philosophy, where law would be recognized in terms of its nonviolent specificity, I propose saying that *war* is the insistent theme of political philosophy and *peace* that of the philosophy of law. If, in fact, conflict, and therefore, in some sense, violence, remains the occasion for judicial intervention, this can be defined by the set of means by which the conflict is raised to the rank of a trial process, this latter being in turn centered on a debate in words, whose initial incertitude is finally decided by a speech act that says what the law is and how it applies. Therefore there exists a place within society—however violent society may remain owing to its origin or to custom—where words do win out over violence. Yes, the parties to a trial do not necessarily leave the courtroom pacified. For that, they would have to be reconciled, they would have to have cov-

---

2. Cf. the essays collected under the heading "Le paradoxe politique," in ibid., 13–158.

ered the path of mutual recognition to its end. As I say, under the straightforward title "The Act of Judging," in my lecture to the Cour de Cassation, the court of appeals in the French legal system, the short-term effect of this act is to decide a conflict—that is, to put an end to uncertainty—whereas its long-term effect is to contribute to social peace—that is, to contribute finally to the consolidation of society as a cooperative enterprise, thanks to those tests of acceptability that go beyond the courtroom and bring into play the universal audience so often referred to by Chaim Perelman.

Of course, I do not want to be misled by the rhetorical dramatization that opposes the political problematic of war to the juridical one of peace. Thus, allow me to suggest in a more careful manner the idea of the intersecting priorities of these two problematics: is peace not also the ultimate horizon of politics thought of as cosmopolitic? And is not injustice, hence finally violence, also the initial situation that law seeks to transcend, without ever fully succeeding? I discuss these questions further in my lecture on the consequences of "sanction" and the disappointments of "rehabilitation."

II

To show that the final peaceful destination of the juridical, to which the judiciary gives particular visibility, is in a way just as originary as is the inclination toward violence exhibited by political evil, even while lacking a demonstration that is without a doubt always beyond proof, it still seems to me that there is at least one eloquent symptom in the testimony of our memory when it seeks to give strength to our first encounters with the question of the unjust and the just. In invoking such childhood memories I deliberately speak of the unjust before the just—just as Plato and Aristotle do so often, and so intentionally. Was not our first entry into the region of lawfulness marked by the cry: "that's not fair"? This is a cry of *indignation,* one whose perspicacity is sometimes confusing when measured against the yardstick of our adult hesitations when summoned to pronounce in positive terms upon the justice or fairness of something. Indignation, in the face of injustice, comes far in advance of what John Rawls calls "considered convictions," whose clash no theory of justice can deny or refuse to consider. Let us recall some of those typical situations where our indignation was aroused. They were, for one thing, those unequal shares that we found unacceptable. (Ah! That model of equal pieces of cake, a model that has perhaps never stopped haunting our dreams of a just distribution, even if it leads to the impasse of a theory of justice!) They were, for another, unkept promises that for the first time shook our innocent confidence in what people said, upon which (we later learned) rested every exchange, contract, and compact. They were also punishments that seemed to us out of proportion with our supposed petty crimes, or praise that we saw arbitrarily given to others rather than ourselves—in short, unmerited retributions. Let us sum up these motives for indignation: disproportionate retributions, betrayed promises, unequal shares. Can we not decipher in them after the fact the lineaments of the juridical order: penal law, the law of contracts and exchanges, distributive justice? What is more, do we not discern in such indignation a precise expectation, that of a word that will create a *just distance* between the antagonists that will bring an end to their head-to-head confrontation? The moral intention of indignation lies in this confused expectation of a victory of the word over violence.

But why then not just hang on to indignation? What does it lack if it is to be equated with an authentic sense of justice? It is not sufficient to say that what is still lacking are the positive criteria of justice. We have still to identify the obstacle that prevents the conquest of what I have just called a "just distance" between antagonists about shares, exchanges, or retributions our indignation denounces as unjust. This obstacle is the desire for vengeance—that is, the claim to obtain justice for oneself, even at the price of adding violence to violence, suffering to suffering. The great conquest, in this respect, consists in separating vengeance and justice. For the short-circuit of vengeance, justice substitutes creating a distance between protagonists, where establishing a difference between the crime and the punishment is the symbol of penal law. How can such a difference be instituted, if not through the addition of a third party who would not be one of the protagonists? An important equation, whereby the just begins to be distinguished from the unjust, proposes itself here: the equation between justice and impartiality. Just distance, the mediation of a third party, and impartiality present themselves as the great synonyms of a sense of justice along the path down which indignation has led us from our earliest youth.

In the preceding pages, I first referred to the motives for my relatively recent desire to withdraw the analysis of the juridical from the tutelage of the ethico-political. Without yet leaving the plane of motivations, I next sought in memories of our youth some testimony to a kind of ontogenetic order leading back to our earliest demands for justice. The moment has come to try to move from these present and past motives to reasons capable of legitimating the intelligible discourse the juridical enterprise presupposes on the unjust and the just. If I have been able, these past few years, to present the reflections you are about to read, at the price sometimes of a certain technical language that will call for the careful attention required by an argumentative discourse, this is because the philosophical *place* of the just was already pointed out and delimited in the "little ethics" of my *Oneself as Another.*[3] In the remainder of this Preface I propose to set out the ties of dependence between the studies you are about to read and the conceptual structures of the three studies comprising that ethics.

III

Readers who are not familiar with that work, in which the essence of my philosophical work can be found, will no doubt appreciate an outline of the three sections of *Oneself as Another* (Studies 7, 8, and 9) that taken together constitute my contribution to moral philosophy.

The architecture of these chapters rests on the intersection of two axes, hence on two different directions of reading. The first axis, which we can call the "horizontal" axis, is that of the *dialogical* constitution of the self (or, as I proposed, of the ipseity that I oppose to mere sameness, in order to characterize the sort of identity that applies to selfhood). The second, "vertical" axis is that of the hierarchical constitution of the *predicates* that qualify human actions in terms of morality. The philosophical *place* of the just thus found itself situated, in *Oneself as Another,* at the intersection of these two orthogonal axes and the two readings they mark out. Let me now try to lay things out somewhat more comprehensively.

---

3. Paul Ricoeur, *Oneself as Another,* trans. Kathleen Blamey (Chicago: University of Chicago Press, 1992).

To begin, let us take up the "horizontal" reading, whose thematic, I have said, is the dialogical constitution of the self. A philosophical theory of the just then finds its first handhold in the assertion that the self only constitutes its identity through a relational structure that places the dialogical dimension above the monological one inherited from the great tradition of reflective philosophy, which is tempted to privilege the latter rather than the former. However, this reference to the other, beginning at the very threshold of a reflection on the constitution of the self, would remain banal and certainly would not suffice to indicate the place where the question of justice can be encountered if, from the beginning, we did not distinguish two distinct senses of the notion of the other or of the other person. The first other, if I may put this way, offers himself through his face, in his voice, with which he addresses me, designating me as the second person singular. This is the other of interpersonal relations. Friendship, opposed in this context to justice, is the emblematic virtue of this immediate relationship that accomplishes the miracle of an exchange of roles between beings that cannot be substituted for each other. You are the you that says "you" to me and to whom I respond, as Emmanuel Levinas loved to repeat, "here I am"—me, in the accusative case. But however wonderful the virtue of friendship may be, it is not capable of fulfilling the task of justice, nor even of engendering it as a distinct virtue. The virtue of justice is based on a relation of distance from the other, just as originary as the relation of proximity to the other person offered through his face and voice. This relation to the other is, if I may so put it, immediately mediated by the *institution*. The other for friendship is the "you"; the other for justice is "anyone," as is indicated by the Latin adage *suum cuique tribuere* (to each his own).

Below, along the second axis of our reading, we shall explore the connotations of this distributive pronoun, found in any conception of society as an enterprise of distributing roles, tasks, benefits, and obligations. In fact, we have already encountered this "anyone" in those exemplary situations in which our youthful indignation lashes out against injustice: unequal shares, failure to keep one's word as given, unfair retributions—all institutional circumstances, in the broadest sense of the term, where justice presents itself as a just distribution. The same thing applies in those infinitely more complex situations where human interactions are caught up in those subsystems that Jean-Marc Ferry, in *Les puissances de l'expérience*,[4] calls "orders of recognition." At each degree of complexity, justice presents itself, in the terms with which John Rawls opens his *Theory of Justice*, as "the first virtue of social institutions."[5] The case of the judicial institution is distinctive in this regard, yet particularly favorable to a narrowed determination of "anyone according to the institution." With the institution of the tribunal, the trial brings into confrontation parties who are constituted as "others" by the judicial procedure. What is more, the institution is incarnated in the person of the judge, who, as a third party between the two parties, takes on the figure of a second-order third party. The judge marks out the just distance the trial establishes between the parties in conflict. True, the judge is not the only one to take on this function of a second-order third party. Without giving way to an excessive penchant for symmetry, we could say that the judge is to the juridical what the teacher of justice is to moral thought, and what the prince, or any personalized figure of sovereign power, is to the political. But it is precisely in the figure of the judge that justice is recognized as "the first virtue of social institutions."

IV

It is only with respect to our second axis—the "vertical" axis—that we can more properly speak of a conceptual architecture having to do with the moral philosophy presented in *Oneself as Another*. The distribution in terms of three levels of predicates, which determine what Charles Taylor, in his *Sources of the Self*,[6] calls "strong evaluations" of action, is so significant that it is what shaped the division of my reflections devoted to morality into three chapters.[7]

At the first level, the predicate that morally qualifies action is the predicate "good." The point of view from which this predicate arises

4. Jean-Marc Ferry, *Les puissances de l'expérience* (Paris: Cerf, 1991).

5. John Rawls, *A Theory of Justice* (Cambridge: Harvard University Press, 1971), 3.

6. Charles Taylor, *Sources of the Self: The Making of Modern Identity* (Cambridge: Harvard University Press, 1989).

7. I hope to show below that the same distribution presided over the order of the texts brought together in this volume, even if the circumstances for which they were produced did not allow me in each case to take into account their eventual place in the hierarchy of levels in my moral philosophy.

can be called teleological inasmuch as the good designates the *telos* of an entire life in quest of what human agents can consider as an accomplishment, a crowning achievement. It is important that the word "life" appears within the framework of a philosophy of action. It recalls that human action is borne by desire, and correlatively by a lack, as well as that it is in terms of these words "desire" and "lack" that we can speak of the wish for a full life. The connections among life, desire, lack, and accomplishment constitute the basis of morality, for which I reserve, as a convention of language, the term "ethics." This is why I define ethics as the wish for a good life.

What does this initial determination of morality in terms of the predicate "good" have to do with an investigation into the just? Simply this: that the three-term relation placed along the horizontal axis discussed above, a relationship wherein each individual mediated by the institution constitutes the third member, finds its initial formulation in the teleological reading of the moral constitution of action. I am making use here again of the formula I proposed in *Oneself as Another:* the wish for a fulfilled life in and with others in just institutions. Justice, for this reading, is an integral part of the wish to live well. In other words, the wish to live in just institutions arises from the same level of morality as do the desire for personal fulfillment and the reciprocity of friendship. The just is first an object of desire, of a lack, of a wish. It begins as a wish before it is an imperative. Here is the mark of a rootedness in life (in the sense of life as *bios* rather than as *zoë*). Certainly, there is no human life that should not be "examined," in the sense of the Socratic adage. And it is the necessity of this examination that, in convergence with the other requirements I shall speak of below, forces it to be raised from the teleological to the deontological point of view. But it remains the case that what calls for such examination is life, the way of leading one's life. The first question in the moral order is not "What must I do?" but rather "How would I like to lead my life?" Aristotle had already indicated that the question of the just belongs to this interrogation when he asserted, at the beginning of the *Nicomachean Ethics,* that the goal of happiness did not reach the end of its trajectory in solitude—to which I would add, friendship—but in the setting of the city. Politics, taken in the broad sense, thus constituted the architectonic of ethics. I would say the same thing in a language closer to that of Hannah Arendt: it is within the *interesse* that the wish for a good life finds its fulfillment. It is as citizens that we become human. The wish to live within just institutions signifies nothing else.

The thesis of the primacy of the teleological approach in the determination of the idea of the just finds an echo in the very composition of the collection of texts brought together here. Without regard for the chronology of their first publication, I have placed at the beginning of this volume two lectures where the emphasis is on the rootedness of the idea of justice in the ground of a philosophical anthropology. The lecture introduced by the question "Who is the subject of rights?" is organized around the idea of capacity, more precisely around the idea of the capable human being (capable of speaking, of acting, of giving an account of him- or herself, of holding him- or herself responsible for his or her acts). The next lecture is devoted more specifically to the latter of these notions, that of responsibility. There I argue that the range of the most recent uses of this term can be unfolded around the pole constituted by the idea of imputation—that is, the idea that action can be assigned to the account of an agent taken to be its actual author. These two ideas of capacity and imputability, dealt with in these lectures without regard for how they go together, take on a new aspect when they are brought together, as I am doing here, under the aegis of a teleological approach to the idea of the just. When set back upon the trajectory of the wish for a good life, they show themselves as constituting the two complementary anthropological presuppositions of an ethics of the just.

V

Let us continue our ascending journey from level to level. After the predicate "good," arising at the teleological level, comes reference to the predicate *obligatory*, on the deontological level. This is the level of the norm, of duty, of interdiction. Just as moral philosophy cannot do without some reference to the good, to the wish for a good life, except at the price of ignoring the rootedness of moral philosophy in life, in desire, in what is lacking, and in what we wish for, so the transition from the wish to the imperative, from desire to interdiction appears to be inevitable. Why? For the fundamental reason that action implies a capacity to do something that gets carried out on the interactive plane as the *power* exercised by an agent *on* another agent who is the recipient of this power. This *power over* others offers the permanent occasion for violence in all its forms: from the lie, where only the instrument of language seems to be misused, to the imposition of suffering, culminating in the imposition of a violent death and in the horrible practice of torture, where the will to humiliate exceeds that of merely imposing suffering. In short, it is owing to the *wrong* that one person inflicts on another that the moral judgment given an action has to add the predicate of the *obligatory* to that of the *good*, usually under the negative figure of what is prohibited. In this respect, an investigation that deliberately aims at the idea of the just must not allow itself to be caught off guard here. What I have already said above about the precedence of the recognition of injustice over the just finds its confirmation and legitimation here. What do we get indignant about, in the case of shares, exchanges, retributions, if not the *wrong* that human beings inflict upon one another on the occasion of the *power-over* one will exercises in the encounter with another will?

But if violence constitutes the primary circumstance in the transition from a teleological to a deontological point of view, it does not take the place of an *argument* in favor of the predicate of the obligatory. Everything remains to be done and to be said concerning the weight of this predicate.

Two remarks made earlier independently of each other may, by being joined, set us on the way to the decisive thesis. I said, in the wake of our reflections on indignation, that it was under the condition of *impartiality* that indignation can free itself of the desire for vengeance that incites the victim to seek to obtain justice for himself. The rule of justice called for in this context, we noted, is incarnated within the figure of the *judge*, considered as a second-order third person. Let us bring these two ideas together. What accounts for the link between the impartiality of judgment and the independence of the judge if not the reference to the law? Here we come to the heart of the deontological point of view. What, in obligation, *obliges* is the claim for universal *validity* attached to the idea of the law.

In *Oneself as Another*, I unfolded the implicit meanings of this claim for universal validity attached to the idea of the law by taking as my guide, for a second time, the threefold relation of what is one's own, what is near, and what is distant. I shall not repeat here my argumentation in a Kantian style by which the threefold relation of the first level allows itself to be rewritten in terms of a second three-fold relation of a second order, which coincides essentially with the three formulations of the Kantian imperative: universalization of the maxim of action, respect for humanity in both myself and the other person, and the establishment of an order of ends whose subjects will at the same time be its legislators. I want instead to concentrate on the important mutation the sense of justice undergoes in passing from the teleological to the deontological point of view. What is centrally at stake here is the *formal* status attached to the universal claim once the law is not just moral but juridical. Let me recall in a few words the thesis I defend in *Oneself as Another*, which I first began to expand in an essay from 1991, reprinted in *Lectures I, autour du politique* under the title "The Just Between the Legal and the Good."[8]

Far from the idea of the just finding on the deontological level a consistency such that it can be removed from any reference to the good (and, as I shall add below, from any recourse to the use of prac-tical wisdom), reasons having to do with the very import of the claim to universality ensure that this claim finds itself held in tension be-tween an indelible reference to the good and the attraction exercised upon it by the purely procedural status of the operations constitutive of legal practice.[9]

In order to make good on my argument, I adopt (provisionally) the description John Rawls gives, in his *Theory of Justice*, of society considered as a vast enterprise for distributing goods—from goods of the market such as remunerations, financial holdings, social benefits; passing through nonmarket goods such as citizenship, security, health, education; to those positions of command, author-ity, or responsibility of every sort exercised within the framework of institutions of every sort. All these goods constitute the stakes for distribution. But such a distribution poses a problem inasmuch as it consists, essentially, in arithmetically unequal shares. The question then is to know whether there exist unequal shares that are more just—or less unjust—than others. Rawls's solution is by now well known. It consists essentially in associating the deontological point

8. This essay is based upon the lecture I gave on March 21, 1991 during the inaugural celebration of the Institut des hautes études sur la justice (the IHEJ).

9. Whence the title "The Just Between the Legal and the Good," which is not repro-duced here owing to its publication in *Lectures I*.

of view with the contractual tradition where recourse to accepted procedures for dividing things reinforces the right decision belonging to the deontological approach in general, without making any reference to the substantial weight of the goods to be distributed. In order to do this, we are to imagine an unreal original situation where the partners, placed by hypothesis in a relation of mutual *fairness,* make one choice, among many, of those principles of justice likely to be accepted by everyone. The procedural operation presiding over the choice of a rule of justice, and consisting in maximizing the smallest of the unequal shares, then results from the conjunction of the deontological point of view and the quite specific form of contractualism bound to the hypothesis of the original situation set within the framework of the fable of the veil of ignorance. The thesis that I propose for discussion, and that I willingly make the second theorem of my theory of the just, following the theorem that the sense of justice is organically bound to the wish for a good life, is that the sense of justice, raised to the level of formalism required by the contractual version of the deontological point of view, cannot be made entirely independent of any reference to the good, owing to the very nature of the problem posed by the idea of a just distribution—namely, taking into account the real heterogeneity of the goods to be distributed. In other words, the deontological level, rightly taken as the *privileged* level of reference for the idea of the just, cannot make itself autonomous to the point of constituting the *exclusive* level of reference.

It is under the aegis of this second theorem that I have chosen to place a number of lectures, the first of which takes up again, in a more critical vein, the question presently under discussion, namely, whether "a purely procedural theory of justice is possible." This is followed by a brief examination of Rawls's work subsequent to *A Theory of Justice,* where he makes more specific the cultural and political conditions in terms of which his theory of justice applies to the practice of democratic societies. Without denying the formal arguments that suffice for the elaboration of a *theory* of justice, the additions and corrections Rawls proposes, with exemplary intellectual probity, will orient my own discussion concerning the conditions for the exercise of justice, which I shall place below under the third point of view of my moral theory, the point of view I place under the aegis of practical wisdom.

It is through a direct confrontation with Rawls's procedural formalism that, in the next lecture, I take up those theories that constitute a plea in favor of a *pluralism* of instances of justice. There I combine the theses Michael Walzer sets out in his *Spheres of Justice,* which in America are representative of what is called "contextualism" or "communitarianism," with those of Luc Boltanski and Laurent Thévenot, who propose another division of the supposedly indivisible idea of justice starting from the idea of *justification* in terms of qualifying tests having to do with economies differentiated by scale.

Another stake besides that of the indivisibility of the idea of justice, inseparable from its formal status, is taken up in these two lectures, namely the question of whether *citizenship*—that is, the modes of belonging to a political body—is itself a good to be distributed, homogeneous with those that have already been briefly mentioned. In this way, the question of *politics* gets reintroduced through a reflection on the just that some have sought to isolate from the tutelage of the problematic of power, sovereignty, violence, and political evil. I do not say that in this way politics takes its vengeance; I simply mean to show that it cannot be forgotten and that its enigmatic character is reinforced by the attempts to align it with the other foci of what we might call juridicity, thanks to a deliberate effort to dissect the unitary idea of justice. The "Juridic," encouraged by a proliferation of kinds of justice, runs aground no less than does the "Political," from which we set out to dissociate ourselves.

The connection is more tenuous between this group of lectures and the one joined to it where I discuss Hannah Arendt's attempt to derive a theory of political judgment from the theory of the judgment of taste Kant set forth in the *Critique of Judgment.* Apart from my oft-expressed admiration for the work of Hannah Arendt, I was led to include this lecture in this volume and in this place by the focus on the "act of judging"—the title Arendt herself chose for the third volume of her important trilogy, *Thinking, Willing, Judging,* unfortunately left unfinished owing to her untimely death. It goes well with the ambition of this collection to recall that the act of judging is not confined to the courts, as my own insistence on making the judiciary the privileged focus of the juridical might suggest. In fact, it is good that a return to the Kant of the third *Critique* brings back into focus for our own examination the problematic of the *re-*

flective judgment, which for Kant himself encompasses, beyond the judgment of taste, the teleological judgment and, by way of it, the whole Kantian philosophy of history. The suggestion therefore arises that the theory of justice could be taken up in another way within a broadly Kantian problematic, if we were to shift our angle of attack from the *Critique of Practical Reason* to that of the *Critique of Judgment.*

VI

In one sense, the group of lectures placed under the third point of view, that of *practical reason,* which in *Oneself as Another* I distinguished from the teleological and the deontological points of view, speaks to this point. In them I wanted to make use of this transition to warn my audience against any tendency to limit my contribution to the discussion of the moral problem, to the opposition between a teleological and a deontological approach. Over against such a reductive move, I would reply that the two studies in *Oneself as Another* devoted to the two levels of moral judgment governed by the predicates of the good and the obligatory (Studies 7 and 8) are merely preparatory exercises for the confrontation that gives me the most difficulty, the confrontation with those situations I place globally under the heading of the *tragic dimension of action.* It is at this stage that the moral conscience, as an inner forum, one's heart of hearts, is summoned to make unique decisions, taken in a climate of incertitude and of serious conflicts. Thus the crucial Study 9 is devoted to the structure of moral judgment in a unique situation in terms of what I call practical wisdom. With this term we return to the Aristotelian virtue of *phronesis,* reinterpreted by Heidegger and Gadamer. In this way, the thesis outlined above that the deontological point of view cannot eclipse the teleological point of view on the level of a general theory of justice finds a complement in the thesis that the just in the final analysis qualifies a unique decision made within a climate of conflict and incertitude. The search for justice ends with a *heartfelt conviction,* set in motion by the wish to live in just institutions, and ratified by the rule of justice for which procedural formalism serves to guarantee impartiality.

If my own reflection on the just has found its privileged reference in the institution of the judiciary, this is because there we can see clearly the need to bring the idea of the just to the final phase of the trial process, where the law is stated here and now. However, we would fall into the opposite error of an exclusive emphasis on formalism if we were to take the problematic of the *application* of the norm as not just a minor point, but as insignificant for any juridical theory worthy of the name. We might be led to such an erroneous misevaluation either by a purely mechanical conception of the application of a norm to a case, or by an overly discretionary conception of the pronouncement of sentence. The whole problem, which I will risk qualifying with the adjective *phronetic,* lies in exploring the *middle* zone where the judgment is formed, halfway between proof, defined by the constraints of logic, and sophism, motivated by the desire to seduce or the temptation to intimidate. This middle zone can be designated by many names, depending on the strategy used: *rhetoric,* to the extent that rhetoric, following Aristotle's definition, consists in giving a "rejoinder" to dialectic, itself understood as a doctrine of probable reasoning; *hermeneutic,* to the extent that this joins application to understanding or explanation; *poetic,* to the extent that the invention of an appropriate solution to the unique situation stems from what, since Kant, we have called the productive imagination, in order to distinguish it from the merely reproductive imagination.[10]

Today I would say that the reflective judgment of Kant's third *Critique* brings together the three aspects distinguished by these three disciplines: probability, subsumption (or application), innovation. Hence the third theorem of the conception of the just unfolded in the lectures collected in this volume will be that the meaning of justice, which conserves its rootedness in the wish for a good life and finds its most ascetic rational formulation in procedural formalism, does not attain concrete plenitude except at the stage of the application of the norm in the exercise of judgment in some situation.

The four lectures that make up the third group of texts assembled here should be seen in light of this theorem. The order in which this group is presented responds to a double preoccupation: that of un-

---

10. See my "Rhétorique, poétique, herméneutique," in *Lectures II: La contrée des philosophes* (Paris: Seuil, 1992), 479–93; "Rhetoric—Poetics—Hermeneutics," trans. Robert Harvey, in *Rhetoric and Hermeneutics in Our Time,* ed. Walter Jost and Michael J. Hyde (New Haven: Yale University Press, 1997), 60–72.

derlining the epistemological specificity of the act of judging, and that of following the unfolding of this act to its conclusion in time.

Thus, in the lecture entitled "Interpretation and/or Argumentation," I link the phase of the hearing, within the framework of the judicial trial, to the problematic I have just placed under the aegis of the reflective judgment. Indeed, it is at this stage of the hearing that we best see *argumentation,* where the logic of the probable predominates, and *interpretation,* where the innovative power of the imagination acts on the very production of arguments, meet and become entangled with each other.

From here, we move, in the next lecture, to the moment where the word that states the law is spoken. This is the moment of the act of judging in the most point-like sense of the term. The judgment has not only a logical import as an act of discourse, but also a moral aspect inasmuch as the ultimate finality of the act of judging, which lies in its contribution to civil peace, goes beyond the finality of the act that brings an end to uncertainty.

However high the stakes in this reflection may be—which brings us back again to our initial considerations on the confrontation between war and peace that takes place at the junction between the juridical and the political—nevertheless I did not want to stop with this dream of peace that constitutes in a way the utopia of the law. In the lecture entitled "Sanction, Rehabilitation, Pardon," I have tried to follow the the act of judging through to its denouement, beyond even the pronouncing of sentence, to the *execution* of the penalty. I wanted in this way to attest that the wish to live in just institutions, and in particular in equitable judicial institutions, will only be satisfied if application is not limited to subsuming a case under a norm, but rather completes its course in the application of the penalty. It seemed to me that it is finally in the measures of rehabilitation, allowing the guilty party to be reestablished in the plenitude of his juridical capacities and the exercise of his citizenship, that the act of judging renders homage to its ultimate end: to reinforce civil peace.

Finally comes the lecture entitled "The Law and Conscience," for the simple reason that the two notions brought together under this title designate respectively the two large problematics into which the theory of justice divides: the problematic of the *self,* in search of its moral identity, and that of the *predicates* presiding over the moral qualification of human action.

For its title I have given this collection of lectures the simple substantive adjective *The Just*. This term applies to persons, actions, and institutions. About all of them, we can say they are just or unjust. Yet from another point of view, that of the level where the *act of judging* is formed, the same predicate can have several senses. On the teleological plane of the wish to live well, the just is that aspect of the *good* relative to something other. On the deontological plane of obligation, the just is identified with the *legal*. It remains to give a name to the just on the plane of practical reason, the one where judgment occurs in a situation. I propose that the just then is no longer either the good or the legal, but the *equitable*. The equitable is the figure that clothes the idea of the just in situations of incertitude and of conflict, or, to put it a better way, in the ordinary—or extraordinary—realm of the tragic dimension of action.

Who Is the Subject of Rights?

I want to show that the question with a juridical form "Who is the subject of rights?" is not to be distinguished in the final analysis from the question with a moral form "Who is the subject worthy of esteem and respect?" (I shall distinguish below between these latter two terms.) Furthermore, the question with a moral form refers in turn to a question of an anthropological nature: "What are the fundamental features that make the self (*soi, Selbst, ipse*) *capable* of esteem and respect?"

This regressive analysis, leading from the concept of right to the moral and from the moral to the anthropological, invites us to concentrate as we begin on the specificity of the question "Who?" in relation to the questions "What?" and "Why?" The question "what?" calls for a description, the question "why?" for an explanation. As for the question "who?" it calls for an identification. It is on the nature of this latter operation, presupposed in every discussion about identity, whether of persons or of historical communities, that I will focus in the first part of my lecture. It is by examining the most fundamental forms of the question "who?" and the responses to it that we are led to give its full meaning to the notion of a *capable* subject. From this, in the second part of the lecture we can turn to consider the ascending order of interpersonal and institutional mediations that assure the transition from the capable subject to the subject of actual rights on the moral, juridical, and political planes.

THE CAPABLE SUBJECT

The notion of capacity will be central to my presentation. It constitutes in my view the ultimate referent of moral respect and of the recognition of a human being as a subject of rights. If such a function can be assigned to a person, it is owing to its intimate connection to the notion of personal or collective identity.

The most direct way to bring out this connection is to consider the different assertions concerning personal or collective identity as all being responses to a series of questions implying the relative pronoun *who*. Who is it that is speaking? Who did this or that action? Whose story (or history) is this? Who is responsible for this injury or this wrong done to another person?

The question "Who is speaking?" is assuredly the most primitive inasmuch as all the others imply the use of language. Only someone capable of designating himself as the author of his utterances can give a response to this question. Examination of this point comes from a pragmatics of discourse, illustrated by the well-known theory of speech acts. Still, we must add to this pragmatics a reflexive prolongation in order to get to the multiple acts of actual utterance by means of which the speaker designates himself or herself as the identical pole or, to use another Husserlian metaphor, the focal point from which radiate an indefinite number of acts of discourse.

The second question about "who" is posed in the same way: Who is the author of an action? I suggested above that the answer to the question "what?" is provided by a description making use of the verbs of action, and that the question "why" is satisfied by an explanation in terms of causes and motives. The question of the attribution of an action to someone is of another order and answers the question "who?" Peter Strawson and H. L. A. Hart speak in this regard of "ascription." I myself would say assignment [*assignation*].[1] The identification of an agent, hence the assignment of an action or of a segment of an action to someone, is often a difficult operation— for example, when one undertakes to evaluate the degree of implication of this or that person in a complex enterprise involving several

---

1. Which in French also has the sense of a summons to appear before a law court.—Tr.

agents. This problem arises constantly on the plane of historical knowledge or in the course of juridical procedures aimed at uniquely identifying the responsible individual who will eventually be forced to compensate an injury or to suffer the penalty for some delinquent or criminal act. As in the preceding case of discourse, the capacity of a human agent to designate himself as the author of his acts has considerable significance for the subsequent assignment of rights and duties. Here we touch upon the heart of the idea of capacity, namely, the ability to do something, what in English is designated by the term *agency*. Unfortunately, our philosophical vocabulary here is quite poor: either we content ourselves with metaphors (the agent, according to one suggestion by Aristotle, is the "father" of his actions, as he is of his children—in both cases, he is their "master"), or we go back to the most primitive usage of the idea of an efficient cause. This latter, expelled from physics since Galileo and Newton, leads back in a way to its birthplace, which is our experience of the power we exercise over our bodily members and, through them, on the course of things. This power of intervention is presupposed by the ethico-juridic concept of imputation, so essential to the assignment of rights and duties.

We advance another step in our exploration of the notion of a capable subject by introducing, along with the temporal dimension of action and of language itself, the narrative component of personal or collective identity. Examining this notion of narrative identity gives us occasion to distinguish the identity of the self from that of things. This latter kind of identity comes down in the final analysis to the stability, even the immutability of a structure, illustrated by the genetic code of a living organism. Narrative identity, in contrast, admits change. This mutability is that of the characters in stories we tell, who are emplotted along with the story itself. This notion of narrative identity is of the greatest importance in inquiry into the identity of peoples and nations, for it bears the same dramatic and narrative character we all too often confuse with the identity of a substance or a structure. At the level of the history of different peoples, as at that of individuals, the contingency of turning points in the story contributes to the overall significance of the story that is told as well as of the protagonists. To recognize this is to free ourselves of a prejudice concerning the identity claimed by different peoples under the heading of arrogance, fear, or hate.

A final stage in the reconstitution of the notion of a capable subject is attained with the introduction of ethical or moral predicates, attached either to the idea of the *good* or to that of *obligation*. (For myself, I want to reserve the qualification "ethical" for the former kind of predicates and "moral" for the latter kind; but our discussion of this point is not directly applicable here.) These predicates apply first of all to those actions we judge and evaluate as good or bad, permitted or forbidden. They further apply reflexively to the agents themselves to whom we impute these actions. It is here that the notion of a capable subject reaches its highest significance. We ourselves are worthy of esteem or respect insofar as we are capable of esteeming as good or bad, or as declaring permitted or forbidden, the actions either of others or of ourselves. A subject of imputation results from the reflexive application to agents of predicates like "good" or "obligatory."

I want to add to these considerations two remarks. First, I would like to suggest that there is a bond of mutual implication between self-esteem and the ethical evaluation of those of our actions that aim at the "good life" (in Aristotle's sense), just as there is a bond between self-respect and the moral evaluation of these same actions, submitted to the test of the universalization of our maxims of action (in the Kantian sense). Taken together, self-esteem and self-respect define the ethical and moral dimension of selfhood, to the extent that they characterize human beings as subjects of ethico-juridical imputation.

I want next to say that self-esteem and self-respect are not simply added to the forms of self-designation we have been considering. They include and in a way recapitulate these forms. In terms of what then, someone may ask, can we esteem or respect ourselves? As, in the first place, capable of designating ourselves as the speakers of our utterances, the agents of our actions, the heroes and narrators of the stories we tell about ourselves. To these capacities are added those that consist in evaluating our actions in terms of "good" and "obligatory." We esteem ourselves capable of esteeming our own actions, we respect ourselves in that we are capable of impartially judging our own actions. Self-esteem and self-respect are in this way reflexively addressed to a capable subject.

THE DIALOGICAL AND INSTITUTIONAL STRUCTURE
OF THE SUBJECT OF RIGHTS

What does the capable subject, whose levels of constitution we have just considered, lack in order to be a *veritable* subject of rights? It lacks the conditions for the actualization of its capacities. These have need of the continual mediation of interpersonal forms of otherness and of institutional forms of association in order to become real powers to which correspond real rights. Let us try to spell this out in greater detail. Indeed it will be helpful, before trying to draw the consequences of this affirmation for political philosophy and the philosophy of right, for us to agree on what we mean by what I have just called the interpersonal forms of otherness and institutional forms of association. Our examination must bear not just on the necessity of a mediation, which we can call mediation of the other in general, but on a division within otherness itself into interpersonal and institutional otherness. It can be tempting for a dialogical philosophy to limit itself to relations with other individual people, which are usually placed under the heading of an I-thou dialogue. It is precisely these relations with other individuals that are held to be worthy of being qualified as interpersonal. But this face-to-face relation lacks the relation to a *third* party that seems just as primitive as the relation to an individual "you." This point is of the greatest importance if we want to account for the transition from the notion of the capable human being to that of the real subject of rights. Only the relation to the third, situated in the background of the relation to the you, gives us a basis for the institutional mediation required by the constitution of a real subject of rights—in other words, of a citizen. This double necessity—that of the mediation by otherness in general and that of the distinction between the other as a "you" and the other as a third party—can be established on the plane of fundamental anthropology to which we appealed in order to elaborate the notion of a capable subject.

At each of the four levels we have considered in succession, we can show the necessity of a triadic constitution governing the passage from capacity to actualization. Let us return to the first level of our anthropological analysis of the capable human being, to the level of the speaking subject. We placed the principal accent on the capacity of the speaker to designate himself as the unique speaker of his multiple utterances. But we pretended to ignore that it is in the context of interlocution that a subject of discourse can identify and designate himself. Within this context, and corresponding to the first-person speaker, there is a second-person hearer of what is said. An utterance, consequently, is at least a bipolar phenomenon, joining an "I" and a "you," whose places can be exchanged, without the persons in question becoming intersubstitutable. Our mastery of the personal pronouns is not complete so long as the rules for this exchange are not fully understood. This mastery contributes in the following way to the emergence of the subject of rights: *like me* the other can designate himself as an *I* when he speaks. The expression "like me" already announces the recognition of the other as my equal in terms of rights and duties. Having said this, we immediately see that this analysis where the other figures only as an individual "you" remains truncated. Not only do we lack the he/she/it of the triad of pronouns (the one or the thing about which one speaks); we lack the reference to the very institution of language in which the interpersonal relation is framed. In this sense, he/she/it represents the institution, inasmuch as it encompasses all the speakers of one natural language who know themselves and who are bound together by the recognition of the common rules that distinguish one language from another. This recognition does not reduce to just the adoption of the same rules by everyone; it also requires the confidence each one of them places in the *rule of sincerity,* without which any linguistic exchange would be impossible. I expect that each will *mean what he or she says.* This confidence establishes public discourse on a basis of trust where the other appears as a third party and not just as a "you." In truth, this fiduciary base is more than an interpersonal relation, it is the institutional condition for every interpersonal relation.

The same triadic relation of me/you/third person can be found on the plane we have distinguished by the question "Who acts?" "Who is the author of an action?" The capacity to designate oneself as the author of one's own actions is inscribed in a context of *interaction* where the other figures as my antagonist or my helper, in relations that vary between conflict and interaction. But innumerable others are implied in any undertaking. Each agent is bound to these others by the intermediary of different orders of *social systems.* We can, with Jean-Marc Ferry, designate with the term "orders of recognition" the large-scale organizations that structure interaction:

technical systems, monetary and fiscal systems, juridical systems, bureaucratic systems, pedagogical systems, scientific systems, media systems, and so on. It is first as one of these systems that the democratic system is inscribed in the sequence of "orders of recognition." (I shall return to this point, which can give rise to a paradox.) That recognition is what is at stake in this organization has to be recalled over against a systematic abstraction that would banish consideration of those initiatives and interventions by which persons posit themselves over against such systems. Conversely, that the organization of social systems is the required mediation for recognition must be affirmed over against a personalist communitarianism that might dream of reconstructing the political bond on the model of the personal bond illustrated by friendship and love.

Some may doubt whether narrative identity presents the same threefold structure as do discourse and action. But they are wrong. Life stories are so intertwined with one another that the narrative anyone tells or hears of his own life becomes a segment of those other stories that are the narratives of others' lives. We may thus consider nations, peoples, classes, communities of every sort as institutions that recognize themselves as well as others through narrative identity. It is in this sense that history, in the sense of historiography, can itself be taken as an institution destined to make manifest and to preserve the temporal dimension of the orders of recognition we have been considering.

We now rejoin the properly ethical level of self-esteem. We have underscored its contribution to the constitution of a capable subject, capable essentially of ethico-juridical imputation. The intersubjective character of responsibility taken in this sense is evident. The example of promises will make it more comprehensible. The other is implicated here in multiple ways: as beneficiary, as witness, as judge, and, more fundamentally, as the one who, in counting on me, on my capacity to keep my word, calls me to responsibility, renders me responsible. The social bond instituted by contracts, by agreements of every sort, which give a juridical structure to the giving of one's word as an exchange, is intercalated within this structure of trust. The principle that agreements should be kept constitutes a rule of recognition that surpasses the face-to-face relation of the promise made between two people. This rule encompasses anyone who lives under the same laws, and, if we invoke international or humanitarian law, humanity as a whole. The other is no longer "you," but the third party designated in a noteworthy way by the pronoun "everyone" [*chacun*], an impersonal but not anonymous pronoun.

We have come to the point where *politics* appears as the setting par excellence for the achievement of human potentialities. The means by which it exercises this function are first set in place by what Hannah Arendt called the "public space of appearance." This expression extends a theme originating in the Enlightenment—that of the "publicity" in the sense of the coming to light of day, without constraint nor dissimulation, of the whole network of alliances within which each human life unfolds its brief history. This notion of a *public space* first expresses the condition of plurality resulting from the extension of interhuman relations to all those that the face-to-face relation of "I" and "you" leaves out as a third party. In turn, this condition of plurality characterizes the will to live together of a historical community—a people, nation, region, class, and so forth—itself irreducible to interpersonal relations. In this sense, the political institution confers a distinct structure on this will to live together that earlier characterized all such systems as "orders of recognition." Again with Hannah Arendt, we can call *power* the common force that results from this will to live together, which only exists so long as this latter will is effective, as the terrifying experiences of defeat, where this bond is undone, give a negative proof. As the word indicates, political power is, across all the levels of power already considered, in continuity with the power by which I have characterized the capable human being. In return, it confers a perspective of endurance over time and of stability on this edifice of powers; more fundamentally, it projects the horizon of public peace understood as the tranquility of order.

It is now possible to pose the question concerning what specific ethical values arise from this properly political level of the institution. We can answer, without hesitation: justice. "Justice," John Rawls writes at the beginning of his *Theory of Justice*, "is the first virtue of social institutions as truth is of systems of thought." But to what does justice stand in relation? Not to the "you" identifiable by your face, but rather to the "everyone" as third person. "To each his own" is its banner. The application to human interactions of the rule of justice presupposes that we can take society as a vast system of distribution, that is, of the sharing of roles, burdens, tasks, well beyond the distribution that takes place on the economic plane of market values. Justice, in this regard, has the same extension as do the "orders of recognition" we spoke of earlier.

I shall not enter here into the discussion of the principle or principles of justice, which would take me far beyond my topic.[2] I will stay instead with the question that began this investigation: who is the subject of rights? We have elaborated two responses. We have said, first, that the subject of rights is the same subject as the subject worthy of respect, and that this subject finds its definition on the anthropological plane in the enumeration of capacities attested to by the answers we give to a series of "who" questions culminating in the question "to whom can human action be imputed?" Next we have given a second response, according to which these capacities would remain virtual, even aborted or repressed, in the absence of interpersonal and institutional mediations, the State figuring a problematic place among these latter.

The first response indicates the correctness of a certain liberal tradition in which the individual precedes the State. The rights attached to the capacities and potentialities we have spoken of constitute, in effect, the rights *of humanity*, in the precise sense of this term—that is, as rights attached to human beings as human beings and not as members of some political community conceived of as the source of positive rights. On the other hand, however, the ultra-individualistic version of liberalism is wrong to the extent that it misconceives the anthropological status of our power to speak, to act, to recount, to impute—in short, the fundamental and multiple *I can* of acting and suffering human existence—and claims to go directly to the actual accomplishments of individuals, which we can admit are contemporary with the positive rights of States. In conclusion, we can see the importance of the distinction between capacity and accomplishment. It governs the distinction between two versions of liberalism. According to one of them, which finds its most noteworthy expression in the tradition of the *social contract*, the individual is already a complete subject of rights before entering into the contractual relation. He gives up real rights that we can call natural rights in exchange for security, as with Hobbes, or for civil status

2. See "Is A Purely Procedural Theory of Justice Possible?" and "After Rawls's *Theory of Justice*" below.

or citizenship, as with Rousseau and Kant. At the same time, his association with other individuals in a political body is insecure and revocable. This is not the case for the other version of political liberalism, which is the one I prefer. Without institutional mediation, individuals are only the initial drafts of human persons. Their belonging to a political body is necessary to their flourishing as human beings, and in this sense, this mediation cannot be revoked. On the contrary, the citizens who issue from this institutional mediation can only wish that every human being should, like them, enjoy such political mediation, which when added to the *necessary* conditions stemming from a philosophical anthropology becomes a sufficient condition for the transition from the capable human being to the real citizen.

The Concept of Responsibility

An Essay in Semantic Analysis

This study is limited in its ambition.[1] I have called it an essay in semantic analysis, or better "conceptual semantics" in the sense Rein-
hart Koselleck gives this term in the field of history and historical
knowledge. This essay is motivated by the sort of perplexity I was left
with following an examination of the contemporary contextual uses
of the term "responsibility." On the one side, this concept seems well
delimited in its classical juridical usage: in civil law, responsibility is
defined by the obligation to make up or to compensate for the tort
one has caused through one's own fault and in certain cases determined by law; in penal law, by the obligation to accept punishment.
We can see the place given to the idea of obligation: an obligation to
compensate or to suffer punishment. A person subject to these
obligations is someone who is responsible. All this seems clear
enough. But, on the other side—or rather, from several other
sides—a kind of vagueness invades the conceptual scene. In the first
place, we are surprised that a term with such a firm sense on the
juridical plane should be of such recent origin and not really well established within the philosophical tradition. Next, the current proliferation and dispersion of uses of this term is puzzling, especially
because they go well beyond the limits established for its juridical
use. The adjective "responsible" can complement a wide variety of
things: you are responsible for the consequences of your acts, but also
responsible for others' actions to the extent that they were done un-

---

1. This text goes with two other texts published in *Esprit:* "Le juste entre le légal et le
bon," *Esprit* 174 (September 1991): 5–21; and "L'acte de juger," *Esprit* 183 (July 1992): 20–25,
the latter of which is included in this volume.

der your charge or care, and eventually far beyond even this measure. At the limit, you are responsible for everything and everyone. In these diffuse uses the reference to obligation has not disappeared, it has become the obligation to fulfill certain duties, to assume certain burdens, to carry out certain commitments. In short, it is an obligation that overflows the framework of compensation and punishment. This overflowing is so forceful that it is under this meaning that the term imposes itself today on moral philosophy, to the point of occupying the whole terrain and of becoming for Hans Jonas, and to a large measure for Emmanuel Levinas, a "principle." This overflowing runs in many directions, thanks to the chance assimilations encouraged by the polysemy of the verb "to respond": not just in the sense of "to answer for . . . " but also as "to respond to . . ." (a question, an appeal, an injunction, etc.). But this is not all. On the properly juridical plane, beyond the extensions referred to above, aimed particularly at what others do or at what a thing under one's care may do—an extension more of the field of application than of the level of meaning—the juridical idea of responsibility is subject to the rivalry of opposed concepts, even newer than the concept under investigation. Mireille Delmas-Marty gives a good summary of these concepts at the beginning of her work *Pour un droit commun,* whether it be a question of danger, risk, or solidarity.[2]

Here then is how things lie: on the one side, a firmness in the juridical definition going back to the beginnings of the nineteenth century; on the other, an absence of attested philosophical ancestry for the same term, an overflowing and displacement of the center of gravity to the plane of moral philosophy, a lively competition among new candidates for the structuring function exercised until now by the concept of responsibility taken in the strict sense of an obligation to pay compensation or to undergo punishment.

Faced with this situation, I propose the following strategy. In the next section, we shall seek, on the side leading to the classical juridical concept of responsibility, the ancestor or founding concept that has its particular place in moral philosophy under a name other than that of responsibility. Then, following from this, in a third section, we shall take account beyond the classical juridical concept of those filiations, derivations, even drifts that lead to the displacements in

2. Mireille Delmas-Marty, *Pour un droit commun* (Paris: Seuil, 1994).

meaning referred to above in the current usage of the term responsibility, as well as the assaults on the properly juridical plane coming from newer rivals. The question in the next section will be to what extent this contemporary, apparently anarchic history will have been rendered intelligible by our investigation into this previous semantic filiation.

BETWEEN IMPUTATION AND RETRIBUTION

The guiding idea in this elucidation of earlier developments is as follows. It is outside the semantic field of the verb "to respond," whether it be a question of answering for or responding to, that we have to seek the founding concept; in fact, we must look in the semantic field of the verb "to impute." A primitive relation to obligation resides within imputation, for which the obligation to compensate or to undergo punishment constitutes only a corollary or complement, which we can place under the generic term "retribution" (or, in the vocabulary of speech-act theory, in the category of "veridictives").

The term "imputation" was well known at a time when that of responsibility was not recognized as having a use outside political theory, where it was a question of the responsibility of the sovereign over against the British parliament. This reference to an extrajuridical use is not uninteresting, inasmuch as the idea appears of giving an account, an idea whose place in the conceptual structure of imputation we shall consider below. This adjacent use of the term responsibility could play a role in the evolution that led to the concept of responsibility, taken in the juridical sense, becoming identified with the moral sense of imputation. But we have not yet reached that point. We need to grasp the concept of imputation in terms of its own structure before interpreting the back-and-forth exchanges between imputation and responsibility.

To impute, say our best dictionaries, is "to put on the account of someone a condemnable action, a fault, therefore an action initially marked by an obligation or a prohibition that this action infringes or breaks." The proposed definition allows us to see how, starting from the obligation or the prohibition regarding some action, and through the intervention first of an infraction, then of a reprobation, the judgment of imputation leads to that of retribution in the sense of an obligation to put things right or to suffer the penalty. But this movement that orients the judgment of imputation toward that of retribution must not lead us to overlook the inverse movement from retribution to the attribution of an action to its author. Therein lies the core of imputation. The *Robert* dictionary cites in this regard an important text from 1771 (the *Dictionnaire de Trévoux*): "to impute an action to someone is to attribute it to him as its actual author, to put it, so to speak, on his account and to make him responsible for it." This definition is worth noting insofar as it makes clear the derivation that leads from attribution to retribution. Let me emphasize this again: to attribute an action to someone as its actual author. We must not lose sight of this reference to an agent. But this is not the only noteworthy thing. The metaphor of an account—"put [the action], so to speak, on his account"—is extraordinarily interesting.[3] It is not at all external to the judgment of imputation inasmuch as the Latin verb *putare* implies calculation, *comput,* suggesting the idea of a kind of moral bookkeeping of merits and demerits, as in a double-entry ledger: receipts and expenses, credits and debits, with an eye to a sort of positive or negative balance—the last offspring of this metaphor must be the very readable and physical demerit book all French drivers carry! In turn, this strange accounting suggests the idea of a kind of moral dossier, or record, as one says in English, a compendium for the inscription of debts and eventually of merits—here again our French police record is very close to the idea of this strange dossier. In this way, we move back to the semimythical figures of the great book of debts: the book of life and death. This metaphor of a balance book seems to underlie the apparently banal idea of being accountable for, and the (apparently even more banal) idea of giving an account, in the sense of reporting, recounting, at the end of a kind of reading of this strange summary dossier.[4]

---

3. It is also noteworthy that other languages, influenced like French by the Latin use of the terms *putare* and *imputatio,* also depend upon the metaphor of an "account," as can be seen in the German *Zurechnung* and the English "accountability." The *Oxford English Dictionary* gives this definition of *accountable:* "liable (*ligabilis,* that can be bound) to be called to account, or to answer to responsibilities and conduct; answerable, responsible." The line from accountable to responsible is preserved in the definition of this latter term: *responsible*—"morally accountable for one's own actions; capable of rational conduct."

4. Until the middle of the nineteenth century, the verb "to impute" could be taken "in large measure" in the sense of attributing (to someone) something praiseworthy or favorable. Attribution can even be done with no idea of praise or blame: to impute a work to its

It is against the background of this turn of phrase within ordinary language, still rich with the metaphor of an "account," that we have to set the attempts to fix the meaning of imputation conceptually.

The contribution of the theology of the Reformation is enlightening in this regard. The key idea is not that of the imputation of a fault, or even of a merit, to the author of an action, but rather the gracious imputation of the merits of Christ, merits acquired on the cross, to the sinner who has faith in this sacrifice. The term imputation—linked to the New Testament Greek *logizethai,* by way of the Latin *imputare*—is in this way absorbed into the gravitational space of the doctrine of justification by faith. The radical basis for this lies in Christ's *justitia aliena* independent of any merit on the sinner's part. In truth, it would be necessary to go even further back, before Luther, to the nominalism of Ockham and the doctrine of *acceptio divina* of John Duns Scotus and, still further, to Saint Paul's interpretation of the faith of Abraham as found in Genesis 15:6. "Abraham believed in God, and . . ." (Romans 3:28; 4:3, 9, 22; Galatians 3:6). Throughout this prehistory of the concept of imputation, the principal accent falls on the way in which God "accepts" the sinner in the name of his sovereign justice or righteousness. It was in this way that the concept of imputation was projected into the conceptual scene at the time of the theological conflicts of the sixteenth century, the Catholic Counter-Reformation rejecting the Lutheran doctrine of justification *sola imputatione justitiae Christi.* Nor should we overlook, from a neighboring order of ideas, in the attempts at a theodicy, the question of the imputation of evil. Having said this, it is a disputed question what the juridical notion of imputability owes to this theological context. The accent placed on "capacity" (*Fähigkeit*) in the notion of *imputativitas* translated into German by *Imputabilität,* then by *Zurechnungsfähigkeit,* or even *Schuldfähigkeit,* suggests a recourse to the Aristotelian concept of a natural disposition, in a direction apparently opposed to Luther's forensic doctrine (in the sense of coming from "outside") of justification. It does not seem illegitimate to take the doctrine of *droit naturel des gens* for a source not

---

presumed author. Whence the expression: to impute a crime or to impute glory. The action of imputing is therefore not necessarily linked to blaming or to accusation, hence to some fault. The theological use of the term, according to which the merits of Christ are attributed to human beings, placed in their account, confirms this.

only independent of but antagonistic to the theological one. With Pufendorf, for example, the principal accent falls on the "capacity" of an agent and not on God's sovereign "justice."[5]

This notion of imputability—in the sense of a (moral and juridical) "capacity of imputation"—constitutes an indispensable key for comprehending the ultimate concern of Kant to preserve the double cosmological and ethical articulation (for which, as we have seen, ordinary language stills bears the imprint) of the term imputation, as a judgment of attribution to someone, as to its actual author, of a blameworthy action. The force of the idea of imputation in Kant consists in the conjunction of two more primitive ideas: the attribution of an action to an agent, and the moral and generally negative qualification of that action. The *Metaphysics of Morals* defines *Zurechnung (imputatio)* in the moral sense as "the judgment by which someone is regarded as the orginator [*Urheber*] (*causa libera* [free cause]) of an action [*Handlung*], which is then called a 'deed' [*Tat*] (*factum*) and stands under laws" (Ak, A, 6, 227).[6] This definition remains unchanged in the Doctrine of Right:

> An action is called a *deed* [*Tat*] insofar as it comes under obligatory laws and hence in sofar as the subject, in doing it, is considered in terms of the freedom of his choice. By such an action the agent is regarded as the author [*Urheber*] of its effect [*Wirkung*], and this, together with the action itself, can be *imputed* to him, if one is previously acquainted with the law by virtue of which an obligation rests on these.
>
> A *person* is the subject whose actions can be *imputed* to him. . . . A *thing* is that to which nothing can be imputed.[7]

However, if we want to reach a more radical level of this cosmological-ethical constitution of the ideas of imputation and imputability in Kant, we must start not with the *Metaphysics of Morals* or the *Cri-*

5. Re this discussion, cf. Ritter, *Imputation (Zurechnung)*, pp. 274–77. For Pufendorf (*De jure naturae et gentium* [Lund, 1672]), see Simone Goyard-Fabre, *Pufendorf et le droit naturel* (Paris: Presses Universitaires de France, 1994), particularly pp. 51–56 relating to the theory of "moral beings" (*entia moralia*), their capacity of institution or imposition (*impositio*), and the relation of imputation that results from this capacity.

6. Immanuel Kant, *The Metaphysical First Principles of the Doctrine of Right*, Part I of *The Metaphysics of Morals*, trans. Mary Gregor (New York: Cambridge University Press, 1996), 19.

7. Ibid., "Introduction," 16 (Ak, 223).

tique of Practical Reason, and not with the Doctrine of Right, but with the *Critique of Pure Reason,* and go directly to the third "Cosmological Antinomy" of the Transcendental Dialectic, where the notion of imputation is placed in an aporetic situation from which it will never really be dislodged.

The terms of this antinomy are well known:

> Thesis: Causality in accordance with laws of nature is not the only causality from which the appearances of the world can one and all be derived. To explain these appearances it is necessary to assume that there is also another causality, that of freedom.
>
> Antithesis: There is no freedom; everything in the world takes place solely in accordance with the laws of nature. (A444–45, B472–73)[8]

Here is where we have to start, with these two ways for an event to happen—either by the effect of things or by the outpouring of a free spontaneity. Of course, it is clear that imputation is meant to apply to the side of the thesis. Here is how it comes into play, first in the *Proof,* then in the *Observation* on this third antinomy. In fact, the word itself does not appear directly in the "proof," only that which constitutes its root, that is, the notion of an "absolute spontaneity of the cause," whereby, it is said, "a series of appearances, which proceeds in accordance with laws of nature, begins *of itself.* This is transcendental freedom."[9] Here is the root: the originary capacity of initiative. The idea of imputability (*Imputatabilität*) introduced in the *Observation* flows from it.

> The transcendental idea of freedom does not by any means constitute the whole content of the psychological concept of that name, which is mainly empirical. The transcendental idea stands only for the absolute spontaneity of an action, as the proper ground of its imputability. This, however, is, for philosophy, the real stumbling block; for there are insurmountable difficulties in the way of admitting any such type of unconditioned causality. (A448, B476)[10]

So imputability, taken in its moral sense, is a less radical idea than that of the "absolute spontaneity of an action." But the price for such

---

8. Immanuel Kant, *Critique of Pure Reason,* trans. Norman Kemp Smith (New York: St. Martin's Press, 1965), 409.

9. Ibid., 411.

10. Ibid., 412.

radicalism is the confrontation with an ineluctably antinomic situation, where two kinds of causality, free causality and natural causality, are opposed to each other with no compromise possible. To which is added the difficulty of conceiving a relative beginning within the course of things, obliging us to dissociate the idea of a "beginning within causality" (which is free causality) from that of a "beginning in time" (the presumed beginning of the world and of reality as a whole).[11]

This is as far as the conceptual analysis of the idea of imputability on the plane of its double cosmological and ethical articulation can go within the framework of the first *Critique*. On the one side, the concept of transcendental freedom remains empty, waiting for its connection with the moral idea of a law. On the other, it is held in reserve as the cosmological root of the ethico-juridical idea of imputability.

It is here that the second *Critique* introduces the decisive connection, that between freedom and law, a connection in virtue of which freedom constitutes the *ratio essendi* of the law, and the law constitutes the *ratio cognoscendi* of freedom. Only now do freedom and imputability coincide.

In what Hegel will subsequently call the "moral vision of the world," the coupling of two obligations—that of acting in conformity with the law and that of compensating for damage done or paying the penalty—tends to be sufficient in itself, to the point of

---

11. What follows in the text of the Dialectic introduces two important ideas. According to the first of these, reason is caught up in this insurmountable controversy through opposed *interests*. First of all, a *practical* interest, which is the one that is dominant in the passage from the idea of a transcendental freedom to that of imputability. (Kant speaks in this regard of the "foundation stones of morals and religion" [A466, B494; p. 424].) But *speculative* interest is just as important, consisting in thinking the unconditioned, irreducible to the movement that the understanding follows in rising and descending from condition to condition. Finally, there is what Kant calls a *popular* interest. "The common understanding finds not the least difficulty in the idea of the unconditioned beginning of all synthesis" (A467, B495; p. 425). On the other hand, empiricism is, not surprisingly, unpopular, for it is difficult for common understanding "to stand silent and to admit its ignorance" (A473, B501; p. 429). The second idea we need to retain for the rest of our discussion is the style of solution to the third antinomy. Whereas the first two antinomies, which are called "mathematical" (concerning the absolute scale of the world in terms of space and time), authorize only a skeptical solution consisting in setting side by side the thesis and antithesis, the "dynamic" antinomy of free and natural causality authorizes a conciliation consisting in conserving the thesis and the antithesis on two distinct planes, that of the finite regression of the chain of conditions leading to the unconditioned and that of the endless regression of conditions.

eclipsing the problematic of cosmological freedom, upon which, however, depends the idea of the attribution of an action to someone as being its actual author. This process of elimination, authorized solely in terms of the *Critique of Practical Reason,* will end up, with Hans Kelsen, for example, in his *Pure Theory of the Law,* at a complete moralization and juridicalization of imputation.[12] At the end of this process, we can say that the idea of retribution (for a fault) has displaced that of attribution (of an action to its agent). The purely juridical idea of responsibility, understood as the obligation to compensate for damages or pay the penalty, can be considered as the conceptual outcome of this displacement. Two obligations remain: that of acting, which the infraction violates, and that of compensation or paying the penalty. Juridical responsibility thus proceeds from the intersection of these two obligations, the first justifying the second, the second sanctioning the first.

THE CONTEMPORARY IDEA OF RESPONSIBILITY: A SHATTERED CONCEPT

In the next part of this essay, I propose to attempt to account for the contemporary restructuring of the idea of responsibility beyond the bounds of this Kantian heritage.

Imputation and "Ascription"

This rather anarchic restructuring, it must be said, was made possible by numerous diverse reinterpretations of the idea of free spon-

---

12. "Imputation designates a normative relation. It is this relation and nothing else that the term *sollen* expresses when it is used in a moral law or in a juridical law" (trans. Ch. Eisenmann, p. 124). What remains then of the cosmological root of imputation as such as it was preserved in the third Kantian antinomy? At the limit, nothing: "It is in no way freedom, understood as the casual non-determination of the will, that makes imputation possible, but just the opposite, imputation presupposes the causal determinability of the will. One does not impute something to man because he is free, but man is free because one imputes it to him" (ibid., 134). I am tempted to say that Kant's second *Critique* has drained the first of its most dramatic part, the theory of antinomies. A final definition of imputation from which every trace of an aporia seems to have been eliminated bears witness to this: imputation, "a connection established between some human behavior and the condition under which it is prescribed or prohibited by a norm" (ibid., 127). I draw these quotations from Simone Goyard-Fabre, *Kant et le problème du droit* (Paris: Vrin, 1975), 47–52.

taneity, preserved by Kant in the background of the moral idea of imputation, as a cosmological idea, although at the price of the antinomy of which we have spoken. These attempts have in common trying to lift the yoke of obligation that, with Kelsen and the whole neo-Kantian school, leads to thoroughly moralizing the sequence constituted by an act, its effects, and the various modes of retribution bearing on those of its effects declared to be contrary to the law. We may speak, in an opposite sense, of a process of demoralization of the root of imputation to characterize attempts to restore the concept of a "capacity" to act, hence of "imputability," whose place we have seen among natural law jurists. If this enterprise were to succeed, the concept of responsibility, which ended up by displacing that of imputability to the point of becoming its synonym and even of replacing it in contemporary vocabulary, might again become available for new adventures, which would not exclude new attempts to remoralize responsibility, but in other ways than in terms of obligation, in the sense of a moral or internalized social constraint. A kind of order may thus result from the comparison between what I am calling an attempt to demoralize the root of imputation and that of remoralizing the exercise of responsibility.

I ask you to excuse the schematic character of this undoubtedly much larger enterprise, which is only meant here to offer the reader an orientation to what is at issue in terms of its broad features.

The reconquest of the idea of free spontaneity has been attempted in various ways which, for my part, I have sought to make converge in a theory of the acting and suffering human being. In this sense, we have on the one hand the contributions of analytic philosophy, and on the other those of phenomenology and hermeneutics.

The former can be divided into the philosophy of language and the theory of action. I shall retain from those analyses stemming from the philosophy of language Peter Strawson's theory of "ascription,"[13] a theory that has influenced such important philosophers of law as H. L. A. Hart, whose well-known article "The Ascription of Responsibility and Rights" is worth recalling at this point.[14] Strawson makes use of the term ascription to designate the predicative op-

---

13. Peter Strawson, *Individuals: Am Essay in Descriptive Metaphysics* (Garden City, N.Y.: Anchor Books, 1963).

14. H. L. A. Hart, "The Ascription of Responsibility and Rights," *Proceedings of the Aristotelian Society* 49 (1948): 171–94.

eration that belongs to a unique genre consisting of attributing an action to someone. His analysis has as its framework a general theory of the identification of "basic particulars," that is, subjects of attribution irreducible to any other, therefore presupposed in every attempt at derivation starting from individuals of an allegedly more fundamental kind. According to Strawson, there are only two such types: spatiotemporal "bodies" and "persons." What predicates do we attribute to ourselves as persons? To answer this question is to define "ascription." Three answers are given: (1) we attribute to ourselves two sorts of predicates, physical predicates and mental/psychic predicates (X weighs sixty kilos, X remembers a recent trip); (2) it is to a single entity, the person, not two distinct entities, say body and mind, that we predicate these two kinds of properties; (3) the psychic predicates are such that they keep the same meaning whether they are attributed to oneself or to another than oneself (I understand jealousy, whether it is said of Peter, Paul, or myself). These three rules of "ascription" conjointly define the person as a "basic particular," both entangled with bodies and distinct from them. There is no need, as regards what is essential, to attach this *sui generis* manner of attribution to a metaphysics of substances. It suffices that we attend to the linguistic rules of identification by "ascription" that cannot be ignored.

The theory of ascription is of interest to us at this stage of our investigation in that among predicates it is those designated by the term *action* that are in fact placed at the center of the theory of ascription. The relation between the action and the agent is thereby covered by such a theory of ascription, that is, the attribution of specific predicates to specific basic particulars, with no consideration of any relation to moral obligation and from the single point of view of the identifying reference to basic particulars. This is why I place the theory of ascription among those attempts that seek to demoralize the notion of imputation.

I am not saying that the theory of ascription is sufficient for a reconstruction of a concept of responsibility less dependent on the idea of obligation, whether it be a question of an obligation to do something or of an obligation to make compensation or suffer a penalty. However, it does have the merit of opening a morally neutral investigation of action. The proof that the theory of ascription constitutes only a first step in this regard is given by the necessity, on linguistic grounds, of completing a semantics of discourse centered on the question of identifying reference, which is acquainted with persons only as things about which one speaks, with a pragmatics of language, where the accent is no longer on statements (their sense and their reference) but on utterances, as in the theory of speech acts: to promise, warn, order, observe, etc. Then it becomes legitimate, as a second stage, to attempt to disentangle the speaker from the utterance, prolonging in this way the process that uncouples the utterance-act from the utterance-proposition. We can then catch hold of the act of self-designation of the speaking subject and the acting subject and make the theory of ascription, which speaks of the person from the outside, combine with a theory of the speaker where the person designates him- or herself as the one who speaks and acts, or even acts in speaking, as is the case in the example of promising, taken as the model for every speech act.

In analytic philosophy, this would be the first half of the organizational plan for a reconstruction of the idea of free spontaneity. The second half would be occupied by the theory of action. Wittgenstein's *Philosophical Investigations* and Donald Davidson's meticulous analyses in his *Essays on Actions and Events*[15] are here the most instructive guides. What it comes down to is that the theory of action has a semantic phase, with its examination of action sentences (Brutus killed Caesar), and a pragmatic phase, with its examination of the ideas of "reasons for acting" and "agency." The examination of this latter notion leads back to an analysis of action close to the Aristotelian theory of *praxis*.

It is at this level—where it is a question of turning to action as a public event, to its intentions and its motives as private events, and from there to the agent as the one who *can*—that we discover unexpected conjunctions and overlappings between analytic philosophy and phenomenological and hermeneutical philosophy.

Indeed, what this comes down to is that it is up to this latter philosophy to take up the question left in suspense by the notion of a self-designation of the subject of discourse and the subject of action. The passage from the utterance to the speaker and that from an action to its agent bring into play a problematic that surpasses the resources of a linguistic philosophy. It is a question of the meaning at-

---

15. Donald Davidson, *Essays on Actions and Events* (Oxford: Clarendon Press, 1980).

tached to answers to the question "who?" (who speaks? who acts? who recounts his life? who designates herself as the morally responsible author of her acts?). The relation of an action to its agent is thus just one particular case, in fact, a highly significant one, of the relation of the self to the ensemble of its acts, whether these be thoughts, words, or actions. This relation is largely opaque to reflection, as is strongly indicated by the metaphors that envelop our attestation of our ability to act. Aristotle, who first undertook a detailed description of "preferential choice" and of "deliberation," had no concept belonging to human action that distinguished human ability to act from the internal principle of physical movement. Actions that "depend on us"[16] are to their agent what children are to their "parents" or what instruments, organs, and slaves are to their "masters." Ever since Locke, modern thinkers have added only one new metaphor, as can be seen in Strawson's theory of ascription when he declares that the physical and psychic predicates of the person "belong to him," that he "possesses" them, that they are "his." This "mineness" of the ability to act does indeed seem to designate a primitive fact, the well-known "I can" so strikingly emphasized, for example, by Merleau-Ponty.

The only way open to a conceptual surpassing of the metaphors of generation, mastery, and possession remains the long route of dealing with the apparent aporias akin to the Kantian antinomy of causality referred to earlier. A pure and simple return to Aristotle is impossible. His philosophy is incapable of making a place for the antinomies of causality that Galilean and Newtonian science has made unavoidable. His philosophy of action is built on a philosophy of nature that remains largely animist. For us, the continuity between natural and free causality is broken. We must pass through the clash of causalities and attempt a phenomenology of their interweaving. What then has to be thought through are the phenomena of *initiative* and *intervention* wherein we can catch sight of the interference of the agent on the course of the world, an interference that effectively causes changes in the world. The fact that we cannot represent to ourselves this hold of the human agent on things within the setting of the course of the world except as a conjunction between several kinds of causality has to be frankly acknowledged as a

---

16. *Ta epli'hemin* (*Nicomachean Ethics*, III, 1112a30–34).

conceptual constraint tied to the structure of action as a kind of initiative, that is, as the beginning of a series of effects in the world. Certainly we have a lively sense, a confident certitude of "being able to act" every time we make an action in our power coincide with occasions for intervention that some finite and relatively closed physical system may offer. But this immediate comprehension, this attestation of an "ability to act" can only be apprehended conceptually as a coincidence of several causalities. Passage through the Kantian kind of antinomy, then the surpassing of this in diverse *ad hoc* models of initiative or intervention[17] has no other function than to bring to a reflective level the assurance attached to the phenomenon of the "I can," the ineradicable attestation the capable human being bears toward him- or herself.

Reformulation of the Juridical Concept of Responsibility

I would like to place under the sign of a redeployment of the concept of responsibility the transformations that get inscribed in the juridical field, on the one hand, and, on the other, those evolutions of moral philosophy that go well beyond the limits of the law.

As concerns the renewal of the idea of responsibility on the juridical plane, I want to emphasize one aspect of the problem that has its origin in civil law, where, as we have already recalled, responsibility consists in the obligation to compensate for damage that has been done. A certain depenalization of responsibility is assuredly already implied in the obligation for simple compensation. We can even then think that beyond the idea of punishment the idea of a "fault" could also disappear. Do we not hold that such a fault is eminently punishable? But this is not the case. The civil code continues to speak of faults in order to preserve, it seems, three ideas—namely, that an infraction has been committed, that the author knows the rule, and finally that he is in control of his acts to the point of having been able to have acted differently. In this way, in classic civil law, the idea of a fault is seen as dissociated from that of punishment, yet it remains attached to that of an obligation to give compensation. But this status today seems conceptually fragile. The recent history of what is

---

17. Among various models of such composition of heterogeneous causalities, I give priority to that of H. von Wright in his *Explanation and Understanding* (London: Routledge & Kegan Paul, 1971).

called the law of responsibility, in the technical sense of the term, has tended to make room for the idea of a responsibility without any fault, under the pressure of concepts such as solidarity, security, and risk, which have tended to take the place of the idea of a fault. It is as though the depenalization of civil responsibility must also imply the complete loss of the sense of culpability.

But can this operation be carried through to its end? The question that arises is whether the substitution of the idea of risk for that of fault does not, paradoxically, end up at a total loss of responsibility for any action. This is why reference to a fault remains ineradicable in the field of civil responsibility. The question has been considered by Mireille Delmas-Marty, in *Pour un droit commun,* as well as by F. Ewald, in *L'État-providence.*[18] One should also look at the article by Laurence Engel, "Vers une nouvelle approche de la responsabilité," in *Esprit.*[19] All these authors start from the assumption that today's crisis in the law of responsibility has its starting point in a shift from the accent previously placed on the presumed author of the damage to a preference for the victim who is placed in a position of demanding compensation for the wrong suffered, which is to say, most often, indemnification. The law of 1898 on accidents at work, which made it obligatory for enterprises to insure themselves against such risks, is seen as the first expression of the transition, with so many implications, "from individual management to a socialized management of risk" (Engel, p. 16). The setting up of a system of indemnification that is both automatic and all-inclusive, observes Engel, "translates the need to see assured an indemnification in the absence of any faulty behavior" (ibid.). The objective evaluation of harm thus tends to obliterate the evaluation of the subjective link between an action and its author. From this is born the idea of responsibility without fault.

We may be pleased with this evolution inasmuch as an important moral value finds itself upheld in this way—namely, that of solidarity, which is assuredly more worthy of esteem than the more utilitarian value of security. But the perverse effects of this displacement ought to put us on guard. They are encouraged by the incredible extension of the sphere of risks and how those risks have changed in

18. F. Ewald, *L'État-providence* (Paris: Grasset, 1986).

19. Laurence Engle, "Vers une nouvelle approche de la responsabilité: le droit français face à la dérive américaine," *Esprit* 192 (June 1993): 5–31.

terms of space and time (Hans Jonas's reflections, to which I shall refer below, start from this very point). At the limit, an acquired incapacity, perceived as a suffered harm, can open to a right to reparation in the absence of any proven fault. The perverse effect consists in the fact that, the more we extend the sphere of risks, the more pressing and urgent is the search for someone responsible, that is, someone, whether a physical or a legal person, capable of indemnifying and making reparation. It is as though the multiplication of instances of victimization gives rise to a proportional increase in what we might well call a social resurgence of accusation. The paradox is immense: in a society that speaks of solidarity, out of a deliberate concern to reinforce a philosophy of risk, the vindictive search for whoever is responsible becomes equivalent to a reintroduction of the culpability of those identified as the authors of any harm done. We need only think of the sarcasm with which public opinion greeted former Minister of Social Affairs Madame Georgina Dufoix's claim, about the scandal over blood tainted with the HIV virus having been given to hemophiliacs, that the officials in charge were "responsible but not guilty."

But there are other, still more subtle effects. To the extent that, in the trial leading to indemnification, it is contractual relations that are at stake in a majority of cases, the suspicion and mistrust that accompany the hunt for whoever is responsible corrupt the capital of confidence upon which rest all the fiduciary systems underlying contractual relations. But this is not all. The virtue of solidarity, invoked on the basis of the exclusive claims of the philosophy of risk, is on the way to being dislodged from its ethically eminent position by the very idea of risk that engendered it, insofar as protection against risk runs in the direction of security rather than toward the affirmation of solidarity. Even more fundamentally, if becoming a victim is unpredictable, its origin also tends to become so thanks to the calculus of probability that places every occurrence under the sign of chance. When so disconnected from a problematic of *decision*, action finds itself placed under the sign of a fatalism that is the exact opposite of responsibility.[20] Fate implicates no one, responsibility someone.

It is in light of these perverse effects that voices are raised today in

20. "There was no chance of an error!"

favor of a more balanced problematic—Mireille Delmas-Marty speaks of "redrawing the landscape"—wherein the imputation of responsibility and the claim for indemnification would be first clearly dissociated in view of being subsequently better coordinated, the idea of indemnification withdrawing to the rank of a management technique aimed at the risk dimension of human interactions. This would make clear the residual enigma of a fault that, kept as part of the background of the idea of responsibility, would not be once more recaptured by the idea of punishment. However, the question remains to what point the idea of a fault can be detached from that of punishment. One way would be to look in the direction of a suggestion, made by (among others) Antoine Garapon, the Secretary General of the Institut des hautes études sur la justice (IHEJ), that the act of stating the law in a determined situation, by setting the accused and the victim in their just place and at a just distance, is valid just as this kind of moral reparation for the victim. But stating the law makes sense only if everyone is *recognized* in terms of his or her role. Do we not here rediscover the hard core of the idea of imputation, as the designation of the "actual" author of an action?

In sum, if there is a need for a "redrawn landscape," it is the landscape of juridical responsibility where solidarity and risk respectively would find their just place.

Transformations of the Moral Concept of Responsibility

The question now is whether other evolutions, transformations, and displacements that have occurred on the moral plane can contribute to this realignment of the concept of responsibility.

A quick glance over the possibilities does not leave much room for hope. What first strikes our eyes is the contrast between the withdrawal on the juridical plane of the idea of imputation, under the pressure of those competing concepts about which I have spoken, and the astonishing proliferation and dispersion of uses of the term responsibility on the moral plane. It is as though the shrinkage of the juridical field were compensated for by an extension of the moral field of responsibility. Nonetheless, for a second look, the paradox seems not so immense as it did at first.

The first inflation to consider is produced on the juridical plane itself. It affects the extension of the domain of risks, accidents, and hazards invoked by victims in a society where every form of harm seems to call for indemnification. As we have already noted in speaking of perverse effects, it is this same inflation that pushes public opinion in the direction of a search for responsible parties capable of making reparation and indemnifying the victims. We can thus legitimately ask whether the presumed inflation of the moral concept of responsibility must not be set in relation to a displacement that finds its origin in juridical responsibility, which places it above an action and its harmful effects, and pushes it more in the direction of required precautions and prudence meant to *prevent* any harm. At the limit, however, we might ask whether there remains, at the end of an evolution where the idea of risk would have conquered the whole space of the law of responsibility, only a single obligation, that of insuring oneself against every risk! In this sense, the jurist extends a hand toward the moral philosopher under the sign of preventive prudence.

This is what the unfolding evolution of the moral idea of responsibility seems to suggest.

I think we ought next to consider the displacement represented by the change in the *object* of responsibility, a displacement that finds expression in new grammatical constructions. On the juridical plane, one declares the author responsible for the *effects* of his or her action and, among them, any harm caused. On the moral plane, it is the *other person, other people* who are held responsible. It is true that this sense is not absent from civil law. The well-known Article 1348, already referred to, says that one is responsible, among other things, for the damage caused "by the acts of persons answerable to one or by things under one's control." The idea of persons for whom one must answer certainly remains subordinated, in civil law, to that of objective damage or harm. Nonetheless, the transference in virtue of which the vulnerable other person or persons tends to replace the harm done as the object of responsibility is facilitated by the intermediary idea of an entrusted responsibility. It is the other *of whom I am in charge* for whom I am responsible. This responsibility no longer comes down to a judgment bearing on the relationship between the author of an action and its effects in the world. It extends to the relation between the agent and the patient (or receiver) of an action. The idea of a person for whom one has responsibility, joined with that of the thing one has under one's control, leads in this way to a quite remarkable broadening that makes the direct object of one's responsibility vulnerable and fragile insofar as it is something handed over to the care of an agent. Responsible for what, one may ask? For what is fragile, one is henceforth inclined to answer. It is true that this displacement and extension were completely unexpected. In an age when the victim, the risk of accidents, and harm done occupy the center of the problematic of the *law* of responsibility, it is not surprising that the vulnerable and the fragile should be equally taken on the *moral* plane for the actual object of responsibility, for the thing for which one is responsible. But we can also give this displacement of the object of responsibility a distinct origin on the moral plane through its connection with the promotion of intersubjectivity as a major philosophical theme. More precisely, if we follow Emmanuel Levinas, it is from others rather than from our inner conscience or heart of hearts that the moral injunction is said to proceed. By becoming the source of morality, other people are promoted to the rank of the object of concern, in respect of the fragility and vulnerability of the very source of the injunction. The displacement then becomes a reversal: one becomes responsible for harm because, first of all, one is responsible for others.

But this not all. Another displacement, which gives a new inflection, is added to this displacement of the object of responsibility, henceforth directed toward vulnerable others, and, through generalization, toward the very condition of vulnerability itself. We can speak here of an unlimited extension in the *scope* of responsibility, the future vulnerability of humanity and its environment becoming the focal point of responsible concern. Let us understand by "scope" the temporal as well as spatial extension given to the notion of the effects of our acts. The question then becomes: how far in space and time does the responsibility for our acts extend? This question takes on its full force when these effects are taken to be harmful toward other humans—in short, as nuisances in the legal sense. How far does the chain of harmful effects of our acts extend that we can take as still implied in the principle, the beginning, the *initium* for which a subject is held to be the author? A partial response is contained in the consideration of the extension of those *powers* exercised by human beings on other human beings and on their common environment. Stated in terms of its scope, responsibility extends as far as our powers do in space and time. The nuisances attached to the exercise of these powers, whether foreseeable, probable, or simply possible, extend just as far as these powers do. Hence a trilogy: powers-nuisances-responsibility. In other words, our responsibility for harm done extends as far as does our capacity to do harm. It is in this way that one can justify, as Hans Jonas does in his *Imperative of Responsibility*,[21] the double relation of responsibility on the one side toward those precautions and the prudence required by what he calls the "heuristic of fear," and on the other toward the potentially destructive effects of our action.

But it is easy to see the new difficulties raised by this virtually unlimited extension of the scope of our acts and therefore of our responsibility. There are at least three ways this happens. First comes the difficulty in identifying who is responsible in the sense of the author properly speaking of any harmful effects. In this way the accepted sense, coming from penal law, of the assignment of a penalty to an individual is called into question. Myriad individual micro-decisions combine to make up an indefinite number of interventions that make sense at the level of instituted systems, whether ecological, bureaucratic, or financial; in short, at the level of all those systems enumerated by Jean-Marc Ferry under the heading "orders of recognition."[22] It is as though responsibility, by expanding its range, dilutes its effects to the point of making the author or authors of harmful effects unknowable. A second difficulty: how far in space and time does the responsibility capable of being assumed by the presumed identifiable authors of such harmful effects extend? The chain of empirical effects of our acts, as Kant observed, is virtually endless. In the classical doctrine of imputation the difficulty is, if not resolved, at least contained within precise limits inasmuch as one only takes into account effects that have already occurred, hence the already identified harmful effects. But what of the harmful effects to come, some of which may not be revealed on a cosmic scale for several centuries? The third difficulty: what becomes of the idea of reparation, even when replaced by that of indemnification, or even of insurance against some risk, when there exists no relation, however extended, of reciprocity between the authors of harmful effects and their victims?

21. Hans Jonas, *The Imperative of Responsibility: In Search of an Ethics for the Technological Age* (Chicago: University of Chicago Press, 1984).

22. See Jean-Marc Ferry, *Les puissances de l'expérience*, vol. 2, *Les ordres de la reconnaissance* (Paris: Cerf, 1991), 7–115.

We can only respond partially to these difficulties. For the retrospective orientation that the moral idea of responsibility has in common with the juridical idea, an orientation thanks to which we are eminently responsible for what we *have done*, must be substituted an orientation that is more deliberately prospective, as a function of which the idea of prevention of future harm will be added to that of reparation for harm already done. With this idea of prevention it becomes possible to reconstruct an idea of responsibility that answers the three concerns we have been considering. We have to say, first of all, that the subject of responsibility is here the same one as the subject who has the power to generate harm, that is, indivisibly individual persons and systems in whose functioning individual acts intervene in a sort of infinitesimal and "homeopathic" way. It is on this small yet real scale that vigilance, the virtue of prudence proper to a prospective responsibility, is exercised. As for the immense scope attributed to our acts by the idea of an effect harmful on a cosmic scale, this can be taken into account if we introduce the succession of generations. Hans Jonas is correct when he, so to speak, interpolates the interhuman tie of filiation between each agent and the long-term effects of his or her actions. Thus there is a need for a new imperative telling us to act in such a way that there will still be humans after us. Unlike the second Kantian imperative, which is aimed at a kind of contemporaneity between the agent and the other person, this imperative does not depend on the span of time in question. Yet (and this will be the response to our third difficulty) a responsibility that does not depend on the span of time in question will also be a responsibility that does not depend on proximity and reciprocity. We might still ask in this case, what becomes of the idea of solidarity when it is so spread over time?

Here new difficulties present themselves, linked to one aspect of the prospective point of view that does not reduce to the prolonging in time of the chain of consequences of action. We must also, and perhaps most importantly, take into account the open conflict between the foreseeable and desired intentional effects of an action and what Robert Spämann calls its "side effects" (in the sense that one speaks of the secondary effects of medication).[23]

23. Robert Spämann, "Nebenwirkungen als moralisches Problem," *Philosophisches Jahrbuch* (1975): 82.

This was, in fact, a problem well known to medieval thinkers, one already referred to by Augustine and then by Abelard in his *Ethica seu Scito teipsum* under the heading *Dolus Indirectus,* at the intersection of the intentional and the unintended.[24] The casuistry of the seventeenth century—including that of Pascal's *Provincial Letters*—did not overlook the dilemma the consideration of secondary effects leads to, for which perverse effects constitute the hardest case. The dilemma can be stated as follows. On the one hand, justification in terms of a good intention alone tends to remove secondary effects from the sphere of responsibility the moment one chooses to ignore them. The precept "to close one's eyes to the consequences" then turns into a kind of bad faith, that of "washing one's hands" of what follows. On the other hand, taking into consideration *every* consequence, including those contrary to the original intention, ends up rendering the agent responsible for everything in an indiscriminate way, which comes down to saying responsible for nothing for which he cannot take charge. As Spämann notes, to take charge of the totality of effects is to turn responsibility into a kind of fatalism in the tragic sense of the word, even into a terrorist denunciation: "You are responsible for everything and guilty of it all!"

Hegel gave a perfect account of this dilemma in the first section of the second part of the *Principles of the Philosophy of Right* devoted to subjective morality *(Moralität).*[25] This framework of the moral vision of the world is not incompatible with the task of making sense of this dilemma. The problem stems, in effect, from the finite character of the subjective will. This finitude consists in the fact that the subjective will can become action only by exteriorizing itself, thus placing itself under the law of external necessity.[26] A number of the effects of our projects on the course of things thus escape the control of our express intention and become entangled with this external

24. Cited by Spämann. The gap between foreseen and unforeseen effects is "constitutive of human action. Human history is one of an ongoing resolution of problems arising from unintended consequences that leave behind them the resolution of past problems."

25. G. W. F. Hegel, *Philosophy of Right,* trans. T. M. Knox (New York: Oxford University Press, 1967), §115–§18, 79–81.

26. "The finitude of the subjective will in the immediacy of acting consists in this, that its action *presupposes* an external object with a complex environment. The deed sets up an alteration in this state of affairs confronting the will, and my will has responsibility in general for its deed [*hat Schuld überhaupt darin*] in so far as the abstract predicate 'mine' belongs to the state of affairs so altered" (ibid., §115, 79).

necessity. Whence the moral dilemma: on the one hand, one would like to impute (*Zurechnen*) to the agent only what follows from an intention that bears the mark (*Gestalt*) of the goal in mind (*Seele*). This intimate connection authorizes extending the predicate "mine" from the intention to the results which, in a way, stem from it and thus continue to *belong* to it. On the other hand, *my* effects do not exhaust what follows as a consequence of the action. Thanks to the connection of willed effects with external necessity, action has consequences that we can say escape the circumspection of the intention. This dilemma means that the maxims "ignore the consequences of an action" and "judge actions by their consequences and make them the criterion of the just and the good" have to be set side by side as maxims of abstract understanding. For how far does the "my" character of "consequences" extend, and where does the "alien" begin?[27] Hegel claims to get out of this dilemma only by surpassing the point of view of morality with that of *Sittlichkeit*, of the concrete social morality that brings with it the wisdom of mores, customs, shared beliefs, and institutions that bear the stamp of history.

The question Hans Jonas poses concerning the extension of our responsibility with regard to future humanity and its environment must, I believe, be placed under the banner of this Hegelian dilemma. But a more complex response than the mere extending to future generations of the Kantian imperative is required. Without simply taking over the Hegelian theory of *Sittlichkeit*, we can affirm, with Robert Spämann, that human action is possible only on the condition of a concrete arbitration between the short-term vision of a responsibility limited to the foreseeable and controllable effects of an action and the long-term vision of an unlimited responsibility. Simply neglecting the side effects of an action would render it dishonest, but an unlimited responsibility would make action impossible. It is surely a sign of human finitude that the gap between intended effects and the uncountable sum of the consequences of any action should itself be unmasterable and comes under that practical wisdom informed by the whole history of previous instances of

27. Of all the consequences of my action, my will has "to accept responsibility [*nur an dem Schuld zu haben*] for only those presuppositions of the deed of which it was conscious in its aim and those aspects of the deed which were contained in its purpose" (ibid., §117). My will "has the right to repudiate the imputation of all consequences except the first, since it alone was purposed" (§118, 80).

such arbitration. Between fleeing responsibility for the consequences and an inflation to an infinite responsibility we must find the just measure and repeat with Spämann the Greek precept: "nothing in excess."

It is with this latter perplexity that I shall end my inquiry. To conclude, let us ask simply what might be the effects of the developments I have described for our earlier discussion concerning the law of responsibility. I am tempted to say: ambiguous ones.

On the one hand, the displacement of the object of responsibility to vulnerable and fragile others incontestably tends to reinforce the pole of imputation in the pair singular imputation–shared risk. To the extent that one is rendered responsible by the moral injunction coming from others, the arrow of such an injunction is directed at a subject capable of designating himself as the author of his acts. A limit is thereby set on the socialization of risks and the anonymous mutual sharing of indemnities.

On the other hand, the extension and especially the prolonging in time of the scope of responsibility may have an opposite effect insofar as the subject of responsibility becomes ungraspable due to its being multiplied and diluted. What is more, when the gap in time between a harmful action and its harmful effects removes all meaning from the idea of reparation, this tends to reinforce the pole of socializing risks at the cost of that of the imputation of action. However, we can also say that once the idea of precaution has been substituted for that of reparation, the subject is then once again assigned responsibility by the call for the virtue of prudence. May we not also say that, far from being polar opposites, imputation and risk overlap and mutually reinforce each other to the extent that, in a preventive conception of responsibility, it is the uncovered risks that are imputable to us?

Finally, it is to the virtue of prudence that we are led once more by the dilemma arising from the question of the side effects of action, among which fall its harmful effects. But it is then no longer a question of prudence in the weak sense of prevention, but one of *prudentia,* heir to the Greek virtue of *phronesis;* in other words, the sense of moral judgment in some specific circumstance. It is to such prudence, in the strong sense of the word, that is assigned the task of recognizing among the innumerable consequences of action those for which we can legitimately be held responsible, in the name of an ethic of the mean. It is in the end this appeal to judgment that constitutes the strongest plea in favor of maintaining the idea of imputability in the face of the assaults from those of solidarity and of risk. If this last suggestion makes sense, then the theoreticians of the law of responsibility, careful to preserve a just distance among the three ideas of imputability, solidarity, and shared risk, will find support and encouragement in those developments that seem at first sight to derive from an idea of responsibility quite far removed from the initial concept of an obligation to make compensation or suffer a penalty.

Is a Purely Procedural Theory of Justice Possible?

John Rawls's *Theory of Justice*

How do I justify choosing John Rawls's book for an inquiry into the theory of justice?[1]

I have two principal reasons. First: Rawls clearly situates himself in the line of descent leading from Kant rather than from Aristotle. Let me recall that the theory of justice, as understood by Aristotle as a particular virtue, namely distributive and corrective justice, gets its meaning, like every other virtue, from a teleological framework of thought that sets it in relation with the good, at least as it is understood by human beings. Kant, on the other hand, brought about a reversal in priority to the benefit of justice and at the expense of the good, so that justice gets its meaning within a deontological framework.

Second, whereas with Kant the idea of the just applies first to relations between persons, with Rawls justice applies first to institutions—it is the virtue par excellence of institutions—and only secondarily to individuals and to nation-states considered as individuals on the historical stage. This deontological approach in moral philosophy can maintain itself on the institutional plane only by basing itself on the fiction of a social contract thanks to which a certain collection of individuals are able to move beyond the supposedly primitive state of nature in order to arrive at a state of law. This encounter between a deliberately deontological perspective in moral philosophy and the contractualist current on the plane of institutions constitutes the central problem to which Rawls addresses himself. The question can be posed in the following terms: Is this

1. John Rawls, *A Theory of Justice* (Cambridge: Harvard University Press, 1971).

connection contingent? Is a deontological approach to moral philosophy logically solidary with a contractualist procedure, where virtue applies to institutions rather than to individuals as was the case with the Aristotelian virtue of justice? What sort of bond is there between a deontological perspective and a contractualist procedure?

My hypothesis is that this bond is in no way contingent, inasmuch as it is the goal and function of a contractualist procedure to assure the primacy of the just over the good by substituting the very procedure of deliberation for any commitment concerning an alleged common good. According to this hypothesis, it is the contractual procedure that is supposed to engender the principle or principles of justice. If this is indeed what is principally at stake, the whole problem of justification of the idea of justice turns around the following difficulty: can a contractualist theory substitute a procedural approach for every attempt to ground justice on some prior convictions concerning the good of all, the common good of the *politéia*, the good of the republic or the *Commonwealth*?

It is exactly to this central question that Rawls provides the strongest answer that has been offered in the present day. His goal is to resolve the problem left unsolved by Kant in his *Rechtslehre* (§§46–47): how to pass from the first principle of morality, autonomy, understood in its etymological sense—namely, the freedom one has insofar as one is rational to give oneself the law as the rule for the universalization of one's own maxims of action—to the social contract by means of which a multitude abandons its external freedom in view of recovering it as a member of a republic. In other words, what is the connection between autonomy and the social contract? This connection is presupposed but not justified by Kant.

If Rawls's undertaking is to succeed, we would then have to say that a purely procedural conception of justice can make sense without any presupposition concerning the good and can even free the just from the tutelage of the good first in what concerns institutions and then by implication in what concerns individuals and nation-states considered as individuals.

In order to anticipate what will follow in our discussion, allow me to say that my principal objection will be to say that a moral sense of justice founded on the Golden Rule—"do not do to others what you would not want to happen to you"—is always presupposed by a purely procedural justification of the principle of justice. But we need to understand that this objection is not equivalent to a refutation of Rawls's theory of justice, something that would lack interest and would even be ridiculous. On the contrary, it leads to a kind of indirect defense of the primacy of this moral sense of justice to the extent that Rawls's extraordinary construction borrows its underlying dynamic from the very principle it claims to engender by its purely contractual procedure. In other words, for me, the circularity of Rawls's argument constitutes an indirect plea in favor of the search for an ethical foundation for the concept of justice. Consequently, it is this circularity that will be at stake throughout my investigation of Rawls's theory of justice.

That his *Theory of Justice* posits the primacy of the just over the good is both clear and openly admitted by Rawls. That revival of the contractualist tradition assures this primacy by equating the just with a procedure specifically held to be "fair"—that is, equitable—is what we need now to demonstrate.

The important thing to say at the beginning is that the whole of Rawls's theory is directed against another version of the teleological conception of justice, namely, the utilitarianism that has predominated over the past two centuries in the English-speaking world and that finds its most eloquent advocates in John Stuart Mill and Henry Sidgwick. This point must not be forgotten in the following discussion. When Rawls speaks of a teleological approach, he is not thinking of Plato or Aristotle, who provide little more than the occasion for a few footnotes, but rather the utilitarian conception of justice. Utilitarianism is a teleological doctrine inasmuch as it defines justice by the maximization of the good for the greatest number. As applied to institutions, this doctrine is merely the extrapolation of a principle of choice constructed at the level of the individual, according to which a simple pleasure or an immediate satisfaction ought to be sacrificed to the benefit of a greater but more distant satisfaction. We shall see below in what way Rawls's second principle of justice is diametrically opposed to this utilitarian version of justice: to maximize the minimal share in a situation of unequal shares—a rule called maximin—differs completely from the rule of maximizing the interest of the greatest number.

The first idea that comes to mind is that there is an ethical moat between the teleological conception of utilitarianism and the general deontological conception. In extrapolating from the individual to the social whole as utilitarianism does, the notion of sacrifice takes on considerable weight. It is no longer a private pleasure that is sacrificed, but a whole social layer. Utilitarianism, as one French disciple of René Girard, Jean-Pierre Dupuy, puts it, tacitly implies a sacrificial principle that is equivalent to legitimating the strategy of the scapegoat. The Kantian reply would be that the least favored in an unequal division of advantages must not be sacrificed because he is a person, which is a way of saying that according to the sacrificial principle the potential victim of some distribution would be treated as a means and not as an end in himself. In a sense, this is also Rawls's conviction, as I shall attempt to show below.

But if it is his conviction, it is not his argument. And this is what counts. His book as a whole is an attempt to shift the question of grounds to the profit of a question about mutual agreement, which is the central theme of every contractualist theory of justice. Rawls's theory of justice is undoubtedly deontological insofar as it is opposed to the teleological approach of utilitarianism, but it is a deontology without a transcendental foundation. Why? Because it is the function of the social contract to derive the contents of the principle of justice from a fair procedure without any commitment regarding the objective criteria of the just, at the price, according to Rawls, of ultimately reintroducing some presuppositions concerning the good. The declared goal of *A Theory of Justice* is to give a procedural solution to the question of the just. A fair procedure in view of a just arrangement of institutions, this is exactly what is signified by the title of chapter 1: "Justice as Fairness."

Fairness, in the first place, characterizes the procedure of deliberation that should lead to the choice of those principles of justice recommended by Rawls, whereas justice designates the content of the chosen principles. In this way, the whole book aims at providing a contractualist version of Kantian autonomy. For Kant, the law is the law freedom would give itself if it could remove itself from the inclination of desires and of pleasure. For Rawls, a just institution would be one that a plurality of reasonable and disinterested individuals would choose if they could deliberate in a situation that would itself be fair—a position whose condition and constraints we shall consider in a moment. But first, I want to emphasize that the major slant of this book is to substitute as far as possible a procedural solution for a foundational solution to the question of the just—whence the constructivist, even artificial turn the book shares with the rest of the contractualist tradition. When the just is subordinated to the good, it has to be discovered; when it is engendered by purely procedural means, it has to be constructed. It is not known in advance. It is supposed to result from deliberation in a condition of absolute fairness. In order to dramatize what is at stake, I want to suggest that justice as fairness—as procedural fairness—aims at resolving Rousseau's well-known paradox of the legislator. We read in the *Social Contract:*

> Discovering the rules of society best suited to nations would require a superior intelligence that beheld all the passions of men without feeling any of them; who had no affinity with our nature, yet knew it through and through; whose happiness was independent of us, yet who nevertheless was willing to concern itself with ours; finally, who, in the passage of time, procures for himself a distant glory, being able to labor in one age and find enjoyment in another. Gods would be needed to give men laws.[2]

Justice as fairness can be understood as the earthly solution to this paradox. This formidable ambition may explain the fascination Rawls's work has exercised for over twenty years on both its friends and its enemies.

Following this long introduction, I propose to consider the answers Rawls gives to the following three questions.

1. What assures the fairness in the situation of deliberation from which an agreement may result concerning a just arrangement of institutions? To this question corresponds the imagination of the "original position" and the well-known allegory that accompanies it, that of the "veil of ignorance."

2. What principles will be chosen behind the veil of ignorance? The answer to this question is to be found in the description and interpre-

2. Jean-Jacques Rousseau, *On The Social Contract,* trans. Donald A. Cress (Indianapolis: Hackett, 1987), Book II, chap. 7, 38–39. He also speaks a bit further on two apparently incompatible things in the work of legislation: "an undertaking that transcends human force, and, to execute it, an authority that is nil" (ibid., 40). Shortly thereafter the paradox becomes one of circularity: "The social spirit which ought to be the work of that institution, would have to preside over the institution itself. And men would be, before the advent of laws, what they ought to become by means of laws. . . . [The legislator therefore] must of necessity have recourse to an authority of a different order, which can compel without violence and persuade without convincing" (ibid.). This is why, for Rousseau, the intervention of heaven and the gods is required.

tation of the two "principles of justice" and their being set in the correct order.

3. What argument ought to convince the deliberating parties to unanimously choose the Rawlsian principles of justice instead of, say, some variation of utilitarianism? The answer lies in the so-called maximin argument borrowed from game theory and transposed from its initial application on the economic plane.

Only after having presented these three cardinal theses in as neutral a manner as possible will we be ready to return to the philosophical question posed above, namely, whether and to what extent a purely procedural conception of justice can be substituted for an ethical foundation of our sociopolitical sense of justice.

The Original Position

As already stated, an agreement is fair if the starting point is fair. Consequently, justice understood as fairness rests on the fairness of what Rawls calls the original situation or position. Two things need to be said at the outset. First, this situation or position is not historical, but hypothetical or imaginary.

> Thus we are to imagine that those who engage in social cooperation choose together, in one joint act, the principles which are to assign basic rights and duties and to determine the division of social benefits. (p. 11)

I shall return in the following section to the underlying conception of social justice as a process or a procedure of distribution indicated by the terms "assign" and "determine the division." Here I want to accentuate the fact that "we are to imagine." This leads me to my second introductory remark: "In justice as fairness the original position of equality corresponds to the state of nature in the traditional theory of the social contract" (p. 12). In fact, the original position is substituted for the state of nature inasmuch as it is a position of equality. We recall that for Hobbes the state of nature was characterized as the war of each against all and, as Leo Strauss emphasizes, as a state wherein everyone is motivated by the fear of a violent death. What is at stake for Hobbes is not justice, but security. Rousseau and Kant, without sharing Hobbes's pessimistic anthropology, describe the state of nature as one without law, that is, with no power that can arbitrate among opposed claims. On the other hand, the principles of justice can become the contents of a common choice if and only if the original position is a fair (that is, equal) one. But it can be fair in this sense only in a purely hypothetical situation.

Discerning the constraints the original position has to fulfill, in order to be held equal in every respect, calls for a great deal of speculation, which finds its intuitive support in the fable of the "veil of ignorance"—to which Rawls owes much of his reputation.

The idea can be expressed as follows:

> Among the essential features of this situation is that no one knows his place in society, his class position or social status, nor does anyone know his fortune in the distribution of natural assets and abilities, his intelligence, strength, and the like. I shall even assume that the parties do not know their conceptions of the good or their special psychological propensities. (p. 12)

We might think that this imaginary state of ignorance reintroduces something like Kant's transcendental will, which is also independent of any empirical ground and, as a result, of any reference to ends or values. In short, it is denuded of any teleological implication. But this assimilation is mistaken. According to Rawls, the subject has earthly interests but does not know what they will turn out to be. We could speak in this regard of an intermediate philosophical position between transcendentalism and empiricism, which does not make it easy to give an exact description of what Rawls means by the original position. This opacity is reflected principally in the answers Rawls gives to the question of just what individuals *must know* behind the veil of ignorance so that the choice will bear on actual earthly things; that is, not just on rights and duties, but on the distribution of social benefits. In other words, to the degree that the choice has to do with interests in conflict, the participants placed behind the veil of ignorance must have some knowledge of what it means "to be interested." In effect, there is a problem of justice as soon as an appropriate division of social *advantages* is at issue. Hence those involved must be not just free and rational persons, but persons concerned to advance their own interests. Whence the first constraint imposed on the original position—namely, that each participant should have a sufficient knowledge of the general psychology of humanity as regards its basic passions and motivations. Rawls frankly recognizes that his philosophical anthropology is very close to that of Hume's *Treatise of Human Nature* (Book III) as regards needs, interests, ends, and conflicting claims, including "the interests of a self that regards its conception of the good as worthy of recognition and that advances claims in its behalf as deserving satisfaction" (p. 127). Rawls calls these constraints the "circumstances of justice" (§22).

Second, the participants must know what every reasonable being is presumed likely to want to possess, namely, those *primary social goods* without which the exercise of liberty would be an empty demand. In this regard, it is important to note that *self-respect* belongs to the list of primary goods. In this way, a purely deontological approach to the notion of justice is not stripped of teleological considerations since these are already present in the original situation (§15, "Primary Social Goods as the Basis of Expectations"). In the original situation, individuals do not know what will be their own conception of the good, but they do know that humans prefer to have more rather than less primary social goods.

Third, the choice being among different conceptions of justice, the participants deliberating behind the veil of ignorance must have suitable information concerning the competing principles of justice. They have to know utilitarian arguments and, ironically, they have to know the Rawlsian principles of justice since the choice is not between particular laws but between global conceptions of justice. This is why in Rawls's work the principles of justice are described and interpreted *before* the thematic treatment of the original position. (We shall return in the critical part of this presentation to the problem of what I call the "order of reasons.") The alternatives open to persons in the original position have to be presented in detail and with all their applications (§21, "The Presentation of Alternatives"). The contract consists precisely in ranking the alternative theories of justice.

This is not all. Rawls also wants to add what he calls "the formal constraints of the concept of right," that is, the constraints that hold for every ethical choice and not just for those of justice. *Publicity* is the most important of these. We shall see below that utilitarianism does not allow for this kind of transparency insofar as the sacrificial principle it implies must remain hidden and not public. Because all the participants must be equal in terms of information, the presentation of alternatives and arguments must be public. Another constraint is what Rawls calls the *stability* of the contract, that is, the anticipation that it will be binding in real life, whatever the prevailing circumstances.[3]

To sum up:

(a) The veil of ignorance has a basic purpose, namely, "to set up a fair procedure so that any principles agreed to will be just. The aim is to use the notion of pure procedural justice as a basis of theory" (p. 136). This connection between the imagination of the veil of ignorance and the search for a purely procedural conception of justice must not be underestimated. Procedural justice constitutes a full-blown alternative to substantive justice governed by shared presuppositions concerning the common good.

(b) Procedural justice is justice inasmuch as behind the veil of ignorance *the effects of specific contingencies* are nullified. The veil of ignorance assures the fairness of the starting situation.

(c) Hence the argument continues: "Since the differences among the parties are unknown to them, and everyone is equally rational and similarly situated, each is convinced by the same arguments." Furthermore, "if anyone after due reflection prefers a conception of justice to another, then they all do, and a unanimous agreement can be reached" (p. 139).

So: in the original situation there is a perfect equation between "any one" and "everyone."

WHAT PRINCIPLES OF JUSTICE WOULD BE CHOSEN BEHIND THE VEIL OF IGNORANCE

Before considering in detail the precise formulation of the two principles of justice, let me make two general comments concerning the "subject of justice."

First comment: justice is not initially an intersubjective virtue, one governing bilateral relations; rather, it governs institutions: "Jus-

3. We shall see in the next chapter, devoted to the articles Rawls has published since the publication of *A Theory of Justice*, that it is this requirement of stability that has provided the occasion for modifications to the original theory.

tice is the first virtue of social institutions, as truth is of systems of thought" (p. 3). This opening assertion seems to fit more with the Platonic conception of justice than with that of Aristotle. Justice is a virtue of the whole for Plato (*Republic*, Book IV), whereas in Book B of his *Nicomachean Ethics* Aristotle takes distributive justice to be a particular or partial justice in relation to justice in general, which is nothing other than obedience to the laws of the City. Why partial or particular? First of all, because it is linked to a specific situation, that of the distribution or apportioning of goods, honors, and advantages. Furthermore, the kind of equality proper to justice is not arithmetic but rather proportional equality, that is, an equality between relations: of shares and those who possess them, the relation of one possessor to some share must be equal to that of another possessor to another share. In this way, to the extent that Plato seems more holistic than Aristotle, Rawls seems to continue more in the line of Plato than in that of Aristotle.

My second comment, however, will correct this conclusion: the Rawlsian conception of justice is *both* holistic and distributive. In this way Rawls links up with Aristotle without betraying Plato. The following passage will make clearer what I am trying to say.

> For us the primary subject of justice is the basic structure of society, or more exactly, the way in which the major social institutions distribute fundamental rights and duties and determine the division of advantages from social cooperation. (p. 7)

So the social system is in the first instance a process of distribution, for the distribution of roles, status, advantages and disadvantages, benefits and burdens, obligations and duties. Individuals are partners. They *take part* inasmuch as society distributes *parts* or shares. This conception of society as a distributive process allows us to surmount the classic opposition between a holistic conception of society, like that of Durkheim, and the epistemological individualism of a Max Weber. If this opposition holds in some way, there would be a clear contradiction between the claim that the primary subject of justice is the basic structure of society and the attempt to derive the basic rules of a society from a contract. To the extent that a society is "a cooperative venture for mutual advantage" (p. 4), it has to be represented both as an irreducible whole and as a system of interrelations among individuals. Justice can then be held to be the virtue of institutions, but of institutions aiming to promote the good of those who take part in them. Taking part is not a marginal feature insofar as institutions, on the one hand, have a distributive function, and, on the other hand, individuals are defined as partners. This is why a rational choice must be jointly made in light of a final agreement about the best way to govern society. It also explains in what sense justice as distributive justice can have as its primary subject the basic structure of society. This basic structure is itself a phenomenon of distribution (which renders inoperative the objections posed by Robert-Paul Wolff, who misconstrues distribution as a purely economic phenomenon opposed to production, in a quasi-Marxist style).[4] What is more, to the extent that society is as a system a phenomenon of distribution, it is to that same extent a problematic one, a field of possible alternatives. Since there are several ways to distribute, to apportion advantages and disadvantages, society from the beginning is a consensual-conflictual phenomenon. On the one hand, every allocation can be challenged, especially, as we shall see, in the context of an unequal apportionment. On the other hand, a stable distribution requires a consensus concerning the procedures meant to arbitrate between competing claims. The principles of justice we shall now consider bear on precisely this problematic situation engendered by the requirement for a fair and stable apportionment.

Having said this, we can now consider the two principles of justice. I shall leave aside the definitive and complete formulation that results from the complex demonstration that will be the object of the third part of my presentation. I quote Rawls:

> The first statement of the two principles reads as follows.
>
> First: each person is to have an equal right to the most extensive basic liberty compatible with a similar liberty for others.
>
> Second: social and economic inequalities are to be arranged so that they are both (a) reasonably expected to be to everyone's advantage, and (b) attached to positions and offices open to all. (p. 60)

The first principle, therefore, assures the equal liberties of citizenship (freedom of expression, of assembly, of the vote, of eligibility for public office). The second principle applies to a condition of

4. Robert-Paul Wolff, *Understanding Rawls* (Princeton: Princeton University Press, 1977).

inequality and posits that certain inequalities must be held to be preferable even to an equal apportionment. I read further:

> The second principle applies, in the first approximation, to the distribution of income and wealth and to the design of organizations that make use of differences in authority and responsibility, or chains of command. [Whence the name "difference principle."] While the distribution of wealth and income need not be equal, it must be to everyone's advantage, and at the same time, positions of authority and offices of command must be accessible to all. One applies the second principle by holding positions open, and then, subject to this constraint, arranges social and economic inequalities so that everyone benefits. (p. 61)

Just as important as the content of these principles is the rule of priority that links them to each other. Rawls speaks here of a serial order:

> These principles are to be arranged in a serial order with the first principle prior to the second. This ordering means that a departure from the institutions of equal liberty required by the first principle cannot be justified by, or compensated for, by greater social and economic advantages. (Ibid.)

This idea of a lexical ordering runs head-on against both Marxism and utilitarianism. Rawls calls this order lexical or lexicographic for a simple reason. In a dictionary, the first letter is lexically first, in the sense that no compensation at the level of the subsequent letters can wipe out the negative effect that would result from substituting any other letter for this first letter. This impossible substitution gives an infinite weight to the first letter. Nevertheless the following order is not denuded of sense since the subsequent letters make the difference between two words having the same first letter without making them mutually substitutable for one another. Applied to the theory of justice, this means: no loss of liberty, no matter what the degree, can be compensated for by an increase in economic efficiency. One does not purchase well-being at the expense of freedom. Commentators who have focused on the second principle apart from consideration of this ordering principle have badly misunderstood Rawls. In fact, the lexical ordering operates not just between the two principles but also between the two parts of the second principle. The least favored in economic terms must be held as lexically having priority over all other partners. This is what Jean-Pierre Dupuy calls the antisacrificial implication of Rawls's principle. Anyone who can be considered a victim must not be sacrificed in order to achieve some common good.

Now, why are there two principles—an egalitarian principle and a nonegalitarian one—rather than just one? Because at the economic level the total sum to be shared is not fixed in advance, but depends on the way in which it is shared. Differences in production result from the way the distribution is arranged. In a system of arithmetic equality, productivity can be so low that even the most favored would be injured. There exists a point at which social transfers become counterproductive. It is at this moment that the difference principle comes into play. Rawls thus finds himself caught between two groups of adversaries. On the right, he is accused of egalitarianism (giving absolute priority to the most disfavored). On the left, he is accused of legitimating inequality. Rawls answers the first group: in a situation of arbitrary inequality, the advantages of the most favored would be threatened by the resistance of the poor or simply by the lack of cooperation on their part. As for the second group: a more egalitarian solution would be unanimously rejected because everyone would be losers. The difference principle picks out the most equal situation compatible with the rule of unanimity.

This latter assertion leads to a third question: for what reasons would the partners placed behind the veil of ignorance prefer these principles in their lexical order rather than some version of utilitarianism? Here is where the antisacrificial implication of Rawls's theory of justice comes to the fore, and it is also here that my own argument finds its starting point.

The Argument

The argument has to do primarily with the difference principle. Borrowed from decision theory as applied to a context of uncertainty, this argument is designated by the term "maximin": the partners will choose the arrangement that *max*imizes the *min*imal share. It is difficult here not to transpose an individual psychology into the original situation, say that of a poker player. But this is not possible, for one's private psychology is just what each partner is ignorant of. Hence the sole motivation that remains in the original situation is that of partners committed, with regard to one another, to respecting a contract whose terms have been publicly defined and unanimously accepted. The contract engenders the bond and the commitment constrains them. No one would bind himself if he had any doubt concerning his capacity to fulfill his promise. This motive is all the more constraining in that the agreement is meant to be final and its object is nothing other than the basic structure of society. If two conceptions of justice are in conflict and if one of them makes possible a situation that someone, anyone cannot accept while the other excludes this possibility, then the second will prevail. Rawls's whole effort turns on the demonstration that, for the utilitarian hypothesis, the one holding the least favored position is a sacrificial victim whereas the conception of justice he defends is the only one to make this person an equal partner. This suffices to prove the superiority of the second thesis.

This point can be shown without taking up all the complexities of the maximin argument. In a society that publicly professes Rawls's principles, the least favored will know that their position draws the maximum advantage of the inequalities they perceive. Less important inequalities will still victimize them. As for the most favored, who seem to be less favored than those like them in every known society, they will be convinced by the argument that their relative loss, compared to the more favorable position a less fair distribution would assure them, will be compensated for by the cooperation of their partners, without which their relative privilege would be threatened. In a society that publicly proclaims itself utilitarian, though, the least favored will be in a wholly different situation. They will be asked to consider that the greatest well-being of the whole population is a sufficient reason to legitimate their poor lot. They must accept seeing themselves and being seen by others as the system's scapegoat. In fact, the situation will be even worse than that. A cynically utilitarian system is incapable of satisfying the rule of publicity. The sacrificial principle implied by utilitarianism has to remain hidden if it is to be efficacious. Which is one more reason to reject the utilitarian conception of justice in the original situation.

Discussion

Now I can return to my initial question. Can we substitute a purely procedural conception of justice for an ethical foundation? In the end, this is what is at stake in every contractual theory of justice.

My thesis is that a procedural conception of justice at best provides a rationalization of a sense of justice that is always presupposed. By this argument I do not mean to refute Rawls, only to develop his presuppositions, which seem to me inevitable. I shall proceed in three steps.

(1) Let us first consider the "order of reasons" (to use a Cartesian expression) followed by Rawls's book. In my opinion, what prevails throughout this work is not a lexical order, like the one that functions between the principles of justice, but a circular order that, again according to me, is characteristic of all ethical reflection. The reader may be surprised by the fact that the principles of justice are defined and even developed (§§11–12) before the examination of the circumstances in which the choice is made (§§20–25), consequently before the thematic treatment of the veil of ignorance (§24) and, in an even more significant way, before the demonstration that these principles are the only rational ones (§§26–30). This does not prevent Rawls from characterizing the two principles of justice in advance as the ones that would be chosen in the original situation. In fact, in section 3, Rawls affirms that the principles of justice are

> the principles that free and rational persons concerned to further their own interests would accept in an initial position of equality as defining the fundamental terms of their association. (p. 11)

In this way the theory is posited as a whole, independent of any real serial order leading to the formulation of the two principles, the original situation, the veil of ignorance, and the rational choice. Without this anticipation, one would not be able to identify justice as fairness:

> The original position is, one might say, the appropriate initial status quo, and thus the fundamental agreements reached in it are fair. (p. 12)

This explains the propriety of the title of chapter 1, "Justice as Fairness," which introduces the idea that "the principles of justice are agreed to in an initial situation that is fair" (ibid.). However, we must anticipate more than just the criterion of the original situation. Even its principal characteristics—namely, the idea that the partners have the same interests, but do not know which ones, and moreover that they "are conceived as not taking an interest in one another's interests" (p. 13)—must be conceived in advance.

Such is the strange status of the "order of reasons." On the one hand, the principles of justice are largely defined and interpreted before the proof is given that these are the principles that would be chosen in the original situation. On the other hand, the original agreement has to be anticipated so that the formulation of the two principles acquires relevance. Rawls himself ratifies this circularity. When he introduces the principles of justice for the first time, he observes:

> I shall not state in a provisional form the two principles of justice that I believe would be chosen in the original position. In this section I wish to make only the most general comments, and therefore the first formulation of these principles is tentative. As we go on I shall run through several formulations and approximate step by step the final statement to be given much later. I believe that doing this allows the exposition to proceed in a natural way. (p. 60)

I interpret this statement in the following way. Before the maximin argument, the definition of justice is merely exploratory; after the maximin argument, it is definitive. As a result, we are faced with a linear argument, but one that provides a progressive clarification of the preunderstanding of what justice means.

(2) This first consideration drawn from the formal disposition of the argument leads to the principal argument, namely, that the procedural definition of justice does not constitute an independent theory, but rests on the preunderstanding that allows us to define and interpret the two principles of justice that we ought to be able to prove—if we ever get that far—would be chosen in the original situation, that is, behind the veil of ignorance. This will be the second stage of my own argument.

My objection seems to challenge the whole contractualist school, for which the procedural dimension must be independent of any presupposition concerning the good in a teleological approach to the concept of justice or even concerning the just in a transcendental version of deontology. In this sense, the whole development of *A Theory of Justice* can be understood as one gigantic effort to assure the autonomy of two moments of the argument, namely, the theory of the original position and the reason to choose the two principles rather than any utilitarian version of justice. My thesis is that the circularity prevails over the linearity claimed by the theory of justice in favor of the autonomy of the theoretical core of the work.

Let us first consider the original situation. The constraints that define it are, to be sure, constructed as a thought experiment and create a wholly hypothetical situation with no roots in history and experience. But they are imagined in such a way that they satisfy the idea of fairness that works like the transcendental condition for all of the procedural development. Now what is fairness, if not the equality of partners confronted with the requirements of a rational choice? Do we not have here the sense of an *isotes* according to Isocrates and Aristotle, which in turn implies respect for the other as an equal partner in the procedural process?

This suspicion that a moral principle governs the apparently artificial construction is confirmed by the role exercised in fact by the maximin argument in the whole demonstration. Rawls seems to want to say that the rule of the maximin as such provides an independent foundation for the choice of the two principles of justice, in preference to the utilitarian concept of justice. He presents his argument as a heuristic procedure allowing us to conceive of the two principles as the maximin solution to the problem of social justice. There is, according to Rawls, an analogy between the two principles and the maximin rule for any choice in a situation of uncertainty. At first glance, the argument has a purely rational appearance, giving an ethical conclusion to nonethical premises. But if we look closer at the decisive argument directed against utilitarianism, namely, that it must be ready to sacrifice some unfavored individuals or groups if that is required by the good of the greatest number, I cannot help thinking that we have here an ethical argument disguised as a technical argument borrowed from decision theory in its most elementary form, game theory, where there are winners and losers divested of any ethical concern. The vice of utilitarianism consists precisely in the extrapolation from the individual to society. It is one thing to say that an individual may have to sacrifice an immediate and lesser pleasure in view of a subsequent, greater pleasure, and another to say that the sacrifice of a minority is required for the satisfaction of the majority. Furthermore, the lexical order between the first and second principle and the maximin rule both plead against the legitimacy of this extrapolation from the individual to society taken as a whole. It seems to me that the argument is a moral one. It is directed against what I call, with Jean-Pierre Dupuy, the sacrificial principle, which comes down to the logic of the scapegoat. I say that the argument is a moral argument, and what is more, one of a Kantian type. According to the sacrificial principle, some individuals are treated as means and not as ends in themselves with regard to some alleged good for the whole. In this way we are led back to the second formulation of the categorical imperative and, beyond it, to the Golden Rule: "Do not do to your neighbor what you would not want him to do to you." I have argued elsewhere that the Golden Rule has the advantage over the Kantian formulation of taking into account reference to more than one good.[5] This is also the case with Rawls, who distances himself from Kant on this point. Behind the veil of ignorance the partners know that human beings have interests. They are only unaware of what theirs will be in real life.

This interpretation of the maximin rule as a tacitly ethical argument could have been anticipated from the very beginning of the book, where on the first page we read:

> Justice is the first virtue of social institutions, as truth is of systems of thought. A theory however elegant and economical must be rejected or revised if it is untrue; likewise laws and institutions no matter how efficient and well-arranged must be reformed or abolished if they are unjust. Each person possesses an inviolability founded on justice that even the welfare of society as a whole cannot override. For this reason justice denies that the loss of freedom for some is made right by a greater good shared by others. (p. 3)

Having read these lines, one can ask how it can be possible to maintain simultaneously the recognition of an ethical presupposition and the attempt to free the procedural definition of justice from every presupposition concerning the good and even the just. Is there some mediation between what I shall call (to be brief) the ethical tendency

---

5. Paul Ricoeur, "Ethical and Theological Considerations on the Golden Rule," in *Figuring the Sacred: Religion, Narrative, and Imagination,* ed. Mark I. Wallace, trans. David Pellauer (Minneapolis: Augsburg-Fortress, 1995), 293–302.

and the purely procedural tendency of the Rawlsian theory of justice? This question brings me to the third stage of my discussion.

(3) The sought-for mediation between the ethical presupposition of the theory of justice taken as a whole and the purely technical maximin argument is suggested by Rawls himself in section 4, when he introduces for the first time the notion of the original position. Having said that we must define the principles of justice as "those which rational persons concerned to advance their interests would consent to as equals when none are known to be advantaged or disadvantaged by social and natural contingencies" (p. 19), Rawls makes the following assertion:

> There is, however, another side to justifying a particular description of the original position. This is to see if the principles which would be chosen match our considered convictions of justice or extend them in an acceptable way. (Ibid.)

Let us stop a moment to consider this notion of "considered convictions." It sums up the whole preunderstanding that Rawls calls "intuitive," namely, those moral judgments "in which we have the greatest confidence" (ibid.). Are not these considered convictions ultimately rooted in the sense of justice equivalent to the Golden Rule applied to institutions and no longer to individuals in a face-to-face relation, and moreover to institutions considered from the point of view of their distributive functions? In fact, our sense of injustice is ordinarily more reliable than is our sense of justice. For example, Rawls says, " we are confident that religious intolerance and racial discrimination are unjust" (ibid.). In this regard, R.-J. Lucas begins his excellent book on justice with a chapter titled "Unjust!"[6] The cry of injustice is the cry of the victim, of that victim utilitarianism is ready to sacrifice for the benefit of the general interest. Yet, if our sense of injustice is ordinarily healthy,

> We have much less assurance as to what is the correct distribution of wealth and authority. Here we may be looking for a way to remove our doubts. (p. 20)

Here is where rational arguments go. But these cannot substitute for our considered convictions.

---

6. John Lucas, *On Justice* (New York: Oxford University Press, 1966).

We can check an interpretation of the initial situation, then, by the capacity of its principles to accommodate our firmest convictions and to provide guidance where guidance is needed. (Ibid.)

We can even go so far as to say that the lexical order of the two principles of justice is virtually preunderstood at the level of these considered convictions:

> Thus it seems reasonable and generally acceptable that no one should be advantaged or disadvantaged by natural fortune or social circumstances in the choice of principles. (p. 18)

In this way, the whole apparatus of argumentation can be considered a progressive rationalization of these convictions, once they are infected by prejudices or weakened by doubts. Rawls gives a name to this mutual adjustment of conviction and theory:

> By going back and forth, sometimes altering the conditions of the contractual circumstances, at others withdrawing our judgments and conforming them to principle, I assume that eventually we shall find a description of the initial situation that both expresses reasonable conditions and yields principles which match our considered judgments duly pruned and adjusted. *This state of affairs I refer to as reflective equilibrium.* (p. 94, emphasis added)

We can speak of equilibrium because our principles and our judgments end up by coinciding, and it is the result of reflection since we know the premises from which they are derived. Rawls's whole book can be thus considered as the search for this reflective equilibrium. But if I understand the course of his argument, the kind of circularity the search for reflective equilibrium seems to presume appears to be threatened by the centrifugal forces exercised by the contractualist hypothesis. I have emphasized at the beginning of this presentation the constructivist and even artificial tendency of both the theory of the original position and that of the maximin argument to favor the difference principle. Can we preserve both the relation of fitness between theory and conviction and the complete autonomy of the argument in favor of the two principles of justice? Such is the ambivalence that seems to me to prevail in Rawls's theory of justice. It wants to win on two fields at once, on the one hand by satisfying the principle of reflective equilibrium, and on the other by constructing an autonomous argument introduced by the hypothetical course of reflection. This explains the apparent discord between the declarations at the beginning, which assign a regulative role to our considered convictions, and the strong plea pronounced later in favor of an independent argument, of the type of the maximin rule. It may be the burden of every contractualist theory to derive from a procedure agreed upon by everyone the very principles of justice that, in a paradoxical fashion, already motivate the search for an independent argument.

In the final analysis, this ambiguity has to do with the role of rational arguments in ethics. Can they be substituted for prior convictions thanks to the invention of a hypothetical situation of deliberation? Or is their function instead to clarify in a critical way such prior convictions? Rawls, it seems to me, seeks to have the best of both worlds—that is, to be able to construct a purely procedural conception of justice without losing the security offered by the reflective equilibrium between conviction and theory. For my part, I will say that it is our preunderstanding of the unjust and the just that assures the deontological intention of the self-proclaimed autonomous argument, including the maximin rule. Detached from the context of the Golden Rule, the maximin rule would remain a purely prudential argument characteristic of every exchange relation. The deontological intention, and even the historical dimension, of our sense of justice are not simply intuitive; they result from a long *Bildung* stemming from the Jewish and Christian as well as from the Greek and the Roman traditions. Separated from this cultural history, the maximin rule would lose its ethical characterization. Instead of being quasi-economic—I would say analogous to an economic argument—it would swerve toward a pseudo-economic argument, one deprived of its rootedness in our considered convictions.

But this first suggestion concerning the epistemological status of rational arguments in ethics makes sense only in conjunction with a second one. We cannot do without a critical evaluation of our alleged sense of justice. The task would be to discern what components or what aspects of our considered convictions require a continual eradication of ideologically biased prejudices. This critical labor will have as its first field of application the prejudices that conceal themselves under what moral philosophers have called "specifying premises," for example, the restriction of the principle of justice that over the centuries allowed one to avoid classifying slaves as human beings. Someone may ask whether there is not something purely utopian in having confidence in the capacity of ordinary citizens as regards rationality, that is, their aptitude for putting themselves in the place of another, or, better, transcending their place. But without this act of confidence, the philosophical fable of the original position would be only an unbelievable and irrelevant hypothesis. We have a further reason to think that this surpassing of prejudices, this opening to critical thinking is possible. This reason proceeds from what we said at the outset about the problematic character of a society defined in terms of its distributive function. Such a society is in principle open to a variety of possible institutional arrangements. For the same reason, justice has to be distributive, and it demands a highly refined mode of reasoning, as Aristotle began to work out in distinguishing between arithmetic and proportional equality.

To conclude, in the expression "considered convictions," the epithet "considered" has as much weight as does the substantive term "convictions." In this context, "considered" means open to the criticism of another or, as Karl-Otto Apel and Jürgen Habermas would put it, submitted to the rule of argumentation.

After Rawls's *Theory of Justice*

The first text by John Rawls expressly titled "Justice as Fairness" appeared in 1957. It was on this basis that he developed, layer by layer, the thick volume entitled *A Theory of Justice*, published in 1971. In the following decade, the author took up the criticism addressed to this work, which had stimulated an immense amount of discussion throughout the world. In 1980, a new series of articles began to appear, aimed not at revising the definition of the principles of justice enunciated in the *princeps* work, or the argumentation by means of which these principles would be shown to be those that would be chosen in preference to all others in a situation that would itself be characterized by fairness. The revision had to do solely with the field of application and the means for carrying out a theory that remained essentially unchanged. We may, therefore, without fear hold *A Theory of Justice* to be canonical. Yet one cannot reread it twenty-five years later without being attentive to those points of doctrine that have undergone a kind of autocritique, of which I shall speak further below.

Rawls's goal in *A Theory of Justice*, as he recalled in 1992 in his preface to the French translation of his subsequent writings, was "to generalize and carry to a higher degree of abstraction the traditional doctrine of the social contract."[1] Certainly it is not the second part of this assertion that will be called into question, but the first. Indeed, he had said in the opening lines of the 1971 volume that "justice is the first virtue of social institutions, as truth is of systems of thought."[2]

---

1. John Rawls, *Justice et démocratie* (Paris: Seuil, 1993), 8; cf. *Political Liberalism* (New York: Columbia University Press, 1993), xv.
2. John Rawls, *A Theory of Justice* (Cambridge: Harvard University Press, 1971), 3.

More precisely, its object was the "basic structure of society" (p. 7), that is, not particular institutions or interactions arising in singular situations, but the arrangement of the principal social institutions into a unique system assigning in this way fundamental rights and duties and structuring the apportionment of advantages and burdens that result from social cooperation. It was important, for those criticisms addressed to Rawls, principally by political philosophers writing in Europe, to underscore from the beginning that the social bond presumed as fundamental by Rawls must be characterized by cooperation and not by domination. This will not be unimportant for his interpretation of the thesis in 1985, precisely characterizing the theory of justice as political. But we shall see, when the time comes, what this epithet "political" will then be opposed to. The "basic structure" is thus a synonym for a "scheme of cooperation." Through their structure and their end, institutions converging on the basic structure are actively involved in "a system of cooperation designed to advance the good of those taking part in it" (p. 4). Justice will be taken to be the primary virtue of these structures, it being admitted that what is at stake is the establishing of mutuality among the concerned individuals. This is what Rawls most obviously shares with the contractualist tradition. Through the contract, society is treated straightaway as a mutual congregational phenomenon. This fundamental presupposition has the advantage, from an epistemological point of view, of setting aside the alternative of a holism à la Durkheim or a methodological individualism à la Weber. The social system being characterized in the first place as a process of distribution of rights and duties, of advantages and burdens, we can say indifferently that the basic structure distributes shares or that the concerned individuals take part in the distribution. There is no trace, therefore, in *A Theory of Justice* of the debate that has so long occupied the social sciences on the European continent.

I

Having said this, in what way does *A Theory of Justice* contribute to carrying to a higher degree of abstraction the traditional doctrine of the social contract? Already in paragraph 3, titled "The Main Idea of the Theory of Justice," the principles of justice (of which we will see that there are two, the second being divided again into two subprinciples) are the same principles that free and rational persons concerned to further their own interests would accept in an initial position of equality as defining the fundamental terms of their association (p. 11).

It is this reference of the justice of the principles issuing from deliberation to the *fairness* of the situation, which will subsequently be called the "original situation," that explains the title of chapter 1, "Justice as Fairness." Fairness characterizes the ultimate choice because it first characterized the initial situation. The choice of principles of justice will be fair if the original situation itself is ("the principles of justice are agreed to in an initial situation that is fair" [p. 12]). The fiction of the original situation thus bears the whole weight of the subsequent demonstration. This feature is classic for the whole contractualist tradition. Before stating what the participants know and do not know in the original situation, it is important to emphasize the procedural orientation of the demonstration imposed by this reference to the original situation. Rival conceptions of the "good life" that characterize teleological doctrines are placed in parentheses. Among these is the predominant teleological version in the English-speaking world, utilitarianism, which found its most eloquent advocates in John Stuart Mill and Henry Sidgwick. It is utilitarianism—and practically only utilitarianism—that is taken as representative of the teleological orientation inasmuch as it defines justice by the maximization of good for the greatest number. This rejection sets *A Theory of Justice* straightaway in the class of deontological theories, and more precisely among those stemming from Kant, as will be affirmed in an important article from 1980, "Kantian Constructivism in Moral Theory."[3] This article spells out that what is retained from Kant is not the opposition between the obligation stemming from practical reason and empirical inclination (or, in other words, transcendentalism, as is the case with Habermas), but rather the idea that the just is constructed inasmuch as it proceeds from a reasonable choice, whereas the good is reputed to be found, discovered, inasmuch as it is apprehended intuitively. The parallel

---

3. "Kantian Constructivism in Moral Theory," *Journal of Philosophy* 77 (April 1980): 515–72.

with Kant can hardly be pushed further than what the "Doctrine of Right" itself admits, namely, the close kinship between the self-legislation that defines moral autonomy and the "act by which a people forms itself into a state."[4] This is what Kant himself calls the "legislative authority" that "can belong only to the united will of the people."[5] It is not that the idea of the good ought to be completely absent from a theory where the just has priority over the good. The idea of "primary social goods" holds a privileged place in the plan of things to be distributed and belongs in this sense to the basic structure of society. It is from the distribution procedure that the idea of good is strictly excluded. A fair distribution procedure must be able to be defined without reference to evaluations attached to the characterization of "goods" as advantages and disadvantages allocated to the partners in the contract. I shall return to this point when we take up the principal points of the discussion unleashed by *A Theory of Justice*. But if it is goods that are to be fairly allocated, the fairness of the distribution must owe nothing to their character as good and everything to the procedure of deliberation. When it is subordinated to the good, the just has to be discovered; when it is engendered by procedural means, it is constructed. It is not known in advance. It is supposed to result from deliberation in a condition of absolute fairness. Therefore Rawls's whole effort at reformulation of the social contract is going to bear on the deliberation procedure and the initial condition of fairness. In this way three problems are implied in this reformulation. First problem: what would assure the fairness of the deliberation situation whence could result an agreement concerning a just arrangement of institutions? Second problem: what principles would be chosen in this fictive situation of deliberation? Third problem: what argument could convince the deliberating parties unanimously to choose the Rawlsian principles of justice rather than, let us say, some variation of utilitarianism?

To the first question corresponds the assumption about the original position and the well-known allegory of the "veil of ignorance" that works as a principle of exposition. One cannot insist too much

4. Immanuel Kant, *The Metaphysics of Morals*, trans. Mary Gregor (New York: Cambridge University Press, 1996), 92.
5. Ibid., 91.

on the nonhistorical but rather hypothetical character of this position. In fact, the original position according to Rawls is substituted for the state of nature of the first social contract theorists, insofar as it is defined as a position of equality. We recall that for Hobbes the state of nature was characterized by the war of all against all and, as Leo Strauss has emphasized, as a state wherein everyone is motivated by the fear of a violent death. Therefore what is at stake for Hobbes is not justice but security. Rousseau and Kant, without sharing Hobbes's pessimistic anthropology, describe the state of nature as lawless, that is, with no power to arbitrate between opposing claims. On the other hand, the principles of justice can become the proposition of a common choice if, and only if, the original position is fair—that is, equal. But it cannot be equal except in a hypothetical situation. An enormous amount of speculation is dispensed with by Rawls in this way concerning the conditions under which the original situation can be said to be fair in every regard. The fable of the "veil of ignorance" is meant to take care of these constraints. The principal point has to do with the question of finding out what the individuals behind the veil of ignorance must know in order for their choice to depend on fair distributions of advantages and disadvantages in a real society where, behind such rights, interests are at play. Whence the first constraint: that each partner should have a sufficient knowledge of the general psychology of humanity as regards its fundamental passions and motivations. Rawls frankly recognizes that his philosophical anthropology is quite close to that of Hume in his *Treatise of Human Nature,* Book 3, as concerns needs, interests, ends, and conflicting claims, including "the interests of a self that regards its conception of the good as worthy of recognition and that advances claims in its behalf as deserving satisfaction" (p. 127).

Second constraint: the partners must know what any reasonable being is presumed to want to possess, namely, the primary social goods without which the exercise of freedom would be an empty claim. In this regard, it is important to note that "self-respect" belongs to this list of primary goods. The choice being among several conceptions of justice, the partners must have suitable information concerning the competing *principles* of justice. They must know the utilitarian arguments and, of course, the Rawlsian principles of justice, since the choice is not between particular laws but between global conceptions of justice. The deliberation consists quite precisely in giving a *rank* to the alternative theories of justice. Another constraint: all the partners must have equal information. This is why the presentation of alternatives and arguments has to be *public*. Still another constraint: what Rawls calls the *stability* of the contract, that is, the anticipation that it will be constraining in real life, whatever the prevailing circumstances may be. We shall see below that it is because this constraint seemed sufficiently unreal to him that Rawls reopened the question of the circumstances of application of a supposedly valid contract. All these precautions bear witness to the difficulty of the problem to be resolved, namely,

> the idea of the original position is to set up a fair procedure so that any principles agreed to will be just. The aim is to use the notion of pure procedural justice as a basis of theory. (p. 136)

What the original situation more than anything else must set aside are the contingent effects due as much to nature as to social circumstances, their alleged merit being due according to Rawls to the number of these contingent effects.

Now the second question comes to the fore: what principles would be chosen behind the veil of ignorance? The answer to this question is found in the description of the two principles of justice and in their being placed in the correct order. These principles, we said in the beginning, are principles of distribution. By receiving parts, the individuals become partners in a "cooperative venture." To the degree that society presents itself as a system of distribution, every problematic division is open to equally reasonable alternatives. This is why specific principles are required that assure the fair—and, let us add, stable—character of the procedure capable of arbitrating among competing claims. The principles that will be stated start exactly from this problematic situation engendered by the requirement for a fair and stable distribution.

As for the two principles of justice, they are:

First Principle
Each person is to have an equal right to the most extensive total system of equal basic liberties compatible with a similar system of liberty for all.

Second Principle

Social and economic inequalities are to be arranged so that they are both:

(a) to the greatest benefit of the least advantaged, consistent with the just savings principle, and

(b) attached to offices and positions open to all under conditions of fair equality of opportunity. (p. 302)

These are called the principles of (1) equality, (2a) difference, and (2b) equality of opportunity. The first principle quite clearly assures the equal liberties of citizenship (freedom of expression, of assembly, of the vote, of eligibility for public offices). But why a second principle? It is remarkable that, for Rawls, as no doubt for most moral philosophers before him, it is the scandal of inequality that sets thought in motion. Rawls thinks first of those inequalities that affect initial opportunities at the beginning of life, what we can call "starting positions." He thinks too, of course, of the inequalities tied to the diversity of contributions individuals make to the working of society, to differences of qualification, of competence, of efficacy in the exercise of responsibility, and so on, inequalities that no society can escape or would want to escape. Thus the problem is to define fairness in such a way that these inequalities are reduced to their ineluctable minimum.

Can we speak, with fairness, of *more or less just inequalities,* of inequalities that are less unjust than others? Whence the second principle of justice. In its first part it posits the conditions under which some inequalities must be held as preferable to even greater inequalities, but also to an egalitarian division, whence the name "principle of difference." In its second part, it equalizes as much as possible the inequalities tied to differences in authority and responsibility. In this way the difference principle picks out the most equal situation compatible with the rule of unanimity. Just as important as the content of these principles is the rule of priority that binds them to each other. Rawls speaks here of a serial or lexical order, clashing head-on with both Marxism and utilitarianism. Applied to the principles of justice, the serial or lexical order means that "a departure from the institutions of equal liberty required by the first principle cannot be justified by, or compensated for, by greater social and economic advantages" (p. 61).

Furthermore, the lexical order also applies to the two parts of the second principle. The least favored in economic terms must be lexically prior with respect to all the other partners. This is what J.-P. Dupuy designates as the antisacrificial implication of Rawls's principle. Whoever might be a victim must not be sacrificed to the benefit of some common good. This is the anti-utilitarian point of the Rawlsian theory of justice.

Next comes the third question: for what reasons would the partners placed behind the veil of ignorance prefer these principles in their lexical order instead of some version of utilitarianism? The argument that occupies a considerable portion in *A Theory of Justice* is borrowed from decision theory in a context of uncertainty. It is designated by the term *maximin,* because the partners are thought to choose the arrangement that maximizes the minimal share. This argument finds its full force in the original situation behind the veil of ignorance. No one knows what their place will be in real society. They reason therefore in terms of pure possibilities. But those involved in the contract are all committed to one another thanks to a contract whose terms have been publicly defined and unanimously accepted. If two conceptions of justice are in conflict and if one of them makes possible a situation that someone cannot accept, while the other excludes this possibility, then the second will prevail.

II

Before considering the important revisions to *A Theory of Justice* produced in Rawls's writings from the years 1980–1987, we need to underline on the one hand the aspects of the theory that will subsequently lend themselves to this revision, and on the other hand those Rawls himself will take as lacking precision and argumentative force, or even as frankly mistaken.

1. In the first rank of the former we must place the notation from the beginning of chapter 4 of *A Theory of Justice* concerning the function of what we can speak of not only as preunderstanding, but as the uninterrupted accompaniment played by what Rawls calls our "considered convictions" concerning justice. These convictions must be "considered," for while in certain flagrant cases of injustice (religious intolerance, social discrimination) our ordinary moral

judgment seems sure, we have much less assurance when it is a matter of fairly sharing riches and authority. We must seek, says Rawls, a means to dissipate our doubts. Theoretical arguments then play the same testing role Kant assigned to the rule of the universalization of maxims. The whole argumentative apparatus can thus be considered as a progressive rationalization of these convictions when they are affected by prejudices or weakened by doubts. This rationalization consists of a complex process of mutual adjustment between conviction and theory:

> By going back and forth, sometimes altering the conditions of the contractual circumstances, at others withdrawing our judgments and conforming them to principle, I assume that eventually we shall find a description of the initial situation that both expresses reasonable conditions and yields principles which match our considered judgments duly pruned and adjusted. This state of affairs I refer to as reflective equilibrium. (p. 20)

Before playing a role in the subsequent revision of Rawls's doctrine, this notion of reflective equilibrium gives a specific twist to his demonstration. It is in situations where a certain moral consensus already reigns that are formed what we could call a preunderstanding of the principles of justice. This is what allows them to be stated even before the process of formalization gets under way. True, this does not prevent the whole development of *A Theory of Justice* from constituting a gigantic effort to assure the autonomy of the two moments of the argument, namely, the theory of the original situation and the reason to choose the two principles rather than some utilitarian version. As regards the original situation, all the constraints that define it are constructed as a thought experiment and create a wholly hypothetical situation, with no roots in history or in experience. But they are imagined in such a way that they satisfy the idea of fairness of which we have a foretaste in situations where our moral judgment is already well established. As for the maximin argument, it is, as already stated, a technical argument borrowed from game theory where there are winners and losers regardless of any ethical concern. Yet we can ask ourselves if it is really distinguishable from a subtle form of utilitarianism, such as consequentialism, if it is not originally paired with a moral argument borrowed from our considered convictions, namely, that in any unequal distribution, it is the fate of the least favored that has to be taken as the touchstone for the fairness of that distribution.

Below I shall show in what way the notion of reflective equilibrium was able to serve as a support for the revision of *A Theory of Justice* proposed beginning in 1980. But first we need to say a word about those points of doctrine John Rawls himself has held to be insufficiently argued for, even as untenable. And this is independent, for him, of the criticism coming principally from "communitarians."[6] These latter have essentially objected that they do not see how an "ahistorical" contract, like that concluded in the original situation behind the veil of ignorance, can *bind* a "historical" society. They have generally based their argument on the fact that in the Rawlsian version of contractualism, the "things" to be distributed constitute primary social goods whose very nature as goods must have some influence on the formal rule of distribution. What qualifies these social goods as "good," if not the estimations, the evaluations, which, compared among themselves, reveal themselves to be heterogeneous? It is from this *real* difference among goods invested in things to be distributed (exchangeable and nonexchangeable goods, positions of authority and responsibility) that Michael Walzer concludes the necessity to refer the definitions (which are different in each case) to multiple and competing spheres, each governed by "shared understandings" of concrete communities. If Rawls does not take this objection into account, it is first of all because he thought the distribution rule was sufficiently constraining, on the rational plane, to neutralize the real heterogeneity of goods. But it is also because his idea of the "basic structure of society" required a complete disjunction between this structure and the particular institutions that are effectively tributary to this heterogeneity of goods and their corresponding evaluations. Far therefore from giving in on this point, Rawls has not stopped accentuating the Kantian aspect of his doctrine over against not only utilitarianism or Nozick's libertarianism,[7]

6. Norman Daniels, ed., *Reading Rawls* (New York: Basic Books, 1975); Michael Sandel, *Liberalism and the Limits of Justice* (Cambridge: Harvard University Press, 1982); Charles Taylor, *Philosophical Papers*, 2 vols. (New York: Cambridge University Press, 1985); Michael Walzer, *Spheres of Justice* (New York: Basic Books, 1983).

7. Robert Nozick, *Anarchy, State, and Utopia* (New York: Basic Books, 1974).

but also different versions of communitarianism, as we can see in an essay from 1978, "The Basic Structure as Subject,"[8] and in another from 1980, "Kantian Constructivism in Moral Theory." It is a difficulty similar in appearance to those brought forth by the communitarians; but it is one discerned by the author himself of *A Theory of Justice* in this great work that will lead to the revisions we are going to consider.

The difficulty, declares Rawls, is "internal to *A Theory of Justice* as fairness, namely that its analysis of the stability of a democratic society, in the third part, does not fit with the theory taken as a whole."[9] By stability, Rawls understood, already in 1971, the property of the contract as enduring to bind together several generations, and, in order to do this, to become inscribed in a history where politics, as we have known since Machiavelli, has the ambition to escape the brevity of individual lives, the vicissitudes of human passions, and the volatility of particular interests.

2. It is in order to face up to these difficulties that John Rawls has come, not to change anything in the definition of the principles of justice or in the argument that makes them preferable to every other kind of principle, but to restrict the field of application to a certain type of society, namely, those democracies he calls constitutional or liberal democracies. And this is owing to the limiting conditions that have to do precisely with the history of these societies and that function at the same time as conditions of *receivability* or of *admission* of the abstract principles of the theory of justice and of the arguments in their favor.

(a) In order to understand the nature of this fundamental limitation of the field of application of *A Theory of Justice* it is necessary to speak of the ambition this limitation is meant to reject. This essentially is the claim to take the theory of justice as "comprehensive" (which can be translated into French as *compréhensive* but also could be rendered as *englobant*), that is, valid for every possible society; and for all the institutions subordinate to the basic structure, even for international institutions of a higher rank; and, finally, for every sort of social transaction. The theory of justice of 1971 was, without having

---

8. "The Basic Structure as Subject," *American Philosophical Quarterly* 14 (1977): 159–65.

9. Preface to the French translation of Rawls's essays published under the title *Justice et démocratie*. Cf. *Political Liberalism*, xvii.

explicitly stated it, such a comprehensive theory. In this respect, it entered into competition with other conceptions of the same amplitude, such as Mill's utilitarianism and Kantian transcendentalism, whose claim it is to cover the totality of human interactions and the institutions that frame them. But it also entered into conflict with the conceptions of the "good life" professed by individuals and communities under the aegis of an idea of the Good. This latter consideration is of the greatest importance, for the oft-repeated opposition between the *just* and the *good* may have appeared as being situated at a broader level of generality. Consequently conceptions of the good—those of the ancients, of the medievals, and, closer to us, those of utility theorists of whatever school—are left to their level of encompassing generality, but internal to the rule of justice professed by a certain type of society, that of a constitutional or liberal democracy. In this sense, the opposition between the just and the good ceases being homogeneous and becomes asymmetric. The good is what is taught by comprehensive doctrines professed by specific individuals or communities. The just is the directive principle of constitutional or liberal societies. This asymmetry is what is indicated by the title of the 1985 lecture, "Justice as Fairness, Political Not Metaphysical."[10] "Metaphysical" is here taken as synonymous with "comprehensive," which is quite surprising if one thinks of Kant or Mill. As for "political," it is taken in the restricted sense of "governing constitutional or liberal democracies." Rawls employs these two qualifications indiscriminately, but never separates the second from the first even though liberalism itself can be taken as a comprehensive— hence metaphysical—theory (let us say a vision of the world embracing the totality of human relations, private and public, communal and at the level of the state, national and international) as well as the basic structure of a certain type of society, that of advanced democratic societies. This is why he tries to distinguish political liberalism from that which has to be called metaphysical.

What reasons are advanced in favor of this drastic reduction of the operative field of *A Theory of Justice*? They are essentially historical reasons of two kinds. The first kind pleads for the disjunction we have already spoken of, the second for a new type of positive rela-

---

10. "Justice as Fairness, Political Not Metaphysical," *Philosophy and Public Affairs* 14 (1985): 223–51.

tions between the procedural level of the idea of justice and the substantial plane of religious, philosophical, and moral conceptions professed by the individuals or communities that make up a society. The important essay "The Idea of an Overlapping Consensus" deals with the second type of these reasons. And it is only with this second series of considerations that a complete response will be given to the objection Rawls himself makes concerning the stability of the social contract as laid out in *A Theory of Justice*.

(b) But let us dwell a moment on the reasons we have presented as *negative*. In brief, the major reason for the sort of switch that is made starting in 1978 is of a historical and sociological order. It is the "fact of pluralism." Rawls traces this back essentially to the wars of religion in the Christian West of the sixteenth and seventeenth centuries. These wars imposed as a fact the simultaneous existence of several faith confessions in the same political space. The solution to this unexpiable conflict was, in effect, the conquest of the idea of tolerance, this being understood at first in the sense of a *modus vivendi* as with Hobbes, or let us say as a strategic and practical expedient ("if we no longer want to continue to kill one another, let us mutually tolerate one another"). But the important point is that the idea of tolerance was affirmed as a positive value at a higher rank than religious confessions and other philosophical and moral convictions, irreducible to one another. Certainly, it must be said that historically it was liberalism as a comprehensive philosophy that allowed this decisive step to be taken. But it is precisely the task of a theory of justice, such as Rawls elaborates it, to detach political liberalism from that metaphysical liberalism that remains in competition with other visions of the world, whether they be religious, philosophical, or moral. To Rawls, this task is inevitable insofar as the increasing complexity of the modern world leaves no chance for a substantial vision of the good or of a transcendental vision of the just to serve as the cement of the social bond. The only alternative would be the imposition of a unique vision of the world by a tyrannical regime. In this sense, political liberty, once freed of its "metaphysical" dross by the renewed theory of the social contract, appears as the only reasonable way beyond the alternative of a war of all against all and tyranny. Basically, only a procedural justice can assure the coexistence of rival visions of the world, principally those centered on divergent ideas of the good, as is affirmed in the 1988 essay, "The Priority of Right and the Ideas of the Good."

The argument would be incomplete if we did not join to the political theory of justice its most important corollary concerning the idea of the *person*. This latter is inseparable from the initial idea of the social bond as a scheme for cooperation. Cooperation implies persons concerned to preserve and to augment their advantage. But the idea of a person, like that of justice, has to be split, depending on whether it is determined by the intention of the good or by its tie to institutions governed by the principle of justice. In the first case, one makes use of a "metaphysical" conception of the person; in the second, just a political idea. In *A Theory of Justice,* citizens were considered as free and equal persons, "who regard themselves as ends and the principles they accept will be rationally designed to protect the claims of their person" (p. 180) in a society "conceived of as a system of cooperation designed to advance the good of its members" (p. 178).

In one sense, Rawls's writings from the 1980s do not say anything different: "Society is a system of fair social cooperation between free and equal persons" (*passim*). However, the *free* character of these persons is more closely related to the first principle of justice, and their *equal* character to the second principle. This reduction of the field of significance of person to the citizen of a constitutional democracy is in fact quite "liberating," inasmuch as it only covers the limited domain of the relation to the basic structure of society, in the expansion of the conquest of the idea of tolerance and the condemnation of slavery. The field is left open to every expression of personal and communal life not encoded by this basic institutional relation. Not only do controversies having to do with visions of the world have a free space, but politics is set apart from these controversies through its withdrawal and abstraction. It is this model that modern constitutional democracies approach. It is this model that *A Theory of Justice* formalized without being entirely clear about the limits of the undertaking.

A partial response is given in this way to the internal objection formulated by Rawls himself about the basis for the condition of *stability* of the contract. Speaking negatively, we can say with assurance "that as regards political practice, no general moral conception can provide a publicly recognized concept for a conception of justice within the framework of a modern democratic State" (p. 208). The important term here is "recognized," that is, precisely historically applicable. In fact, the response to the objection is already no longer merely negative. It is already positive if we consider that the second principle of justice, and more precisely the second part of this principle ("social and economic inequalities are to be arranged so that they are . . . to the greatest benefit of the least advantaged"), is addressed to claims for equality raised by rival communities of thinking and assures an institutional protection for the rights, liberties, and opportunities attached to these claims. Liberal democracy is meant precisely for citizens who are in virtual disagreement over what is essential. It undertakes to limit the extent of public disagreement.

We ought not to stop with this excessively modest proposal, however. It is reasonable to propose more and to try to reconstruct a more positive bond between the rule of justice and the depth of beliefs effectively professed in our modern societies. It is the idea of an overlapping consensus that corresponds to this request. It must be said right away that this idea is situated in the very extension of the idea of a reflective equilibrium between the theory and our considered convictions. But *A Theory of Justice* does not say what considered convictions satisfied the conditions for reflective equilibrium. This is because its limitation to the historical field of liberal democracy had not been perceived. Yet *A Theory of Justice* did presuppose among the partners in the social contract the *intuitive* basic idea that citizens are free and equal persons in virtue of precisely their moral capacities, namely, their very sense of justice, that is, "their capacity to understand, apply, and respect in their acts the public conception of justice that characterizes a fair cooperation" (p. 218).

Where does the motivation and, if we may put it this way, the instruction in such a moral capacity come from? It is here that the idea of an overlapping consensus intervenes. Short of this point, the theory of justice only rests on a strategy of *avoiding* controversies, along the lines of the idea of tolerance that ended the wars of religion in the Christian West. Now it is necessary to take a step in the direction of a *wager,* namely that rival "metaphysical" conceptions that have fed and continue to nourish the strong convictions of citizens belonging to Western democracies can motivate, justify, and found the same minimal body of beliefs likely to contribute to the reflective equilibrium required by *A Theory of Justice.* Rawls's article from 1989, bearing precisely the title "The Domain of the Political and Overlapping Consensus," is expressly devoted to this *wager* which parallels the method of avoidance just mentioned. In the first place, it is affirmed that the theory of justice as fairness constitutes an independent political conception, in other words, one not deducible from a general theory of institutions or of community. Therefore it requires a distinct justification, its own guarantee of stability. Only some "comprehensive" doctrines, be they moral, philosophical, or religious, can, despite their mutual opposition, come together through their overlapping as this common foundation of the values belonging to a fair democracy, one that is capable of enduring.

One sees the scope of the wager. This is underlined by the idea complementary to that of an overlapping consensus, namely, the idea of "reasonable disagreement," which constitutes the actual core of this important article.

> We can say that reasonable disagreement is disagreement between reasonable persons, that is, between persons who have realized their two moral powers [these faculties are the capacity to have a sense of justice and a conception of the good] to a degree sufficient to be free and equal citizens in a democratic regime, who have an enduring desire to be fully cooperating members of society over a complete life.[11]

It follows from this statement that the opposition between political and "metaphysical" applied to the idea of justice does not imply any mistrust, or indifference, or hostility with regard to "metaphysical" conceptions of the good inasmuch as it is from their agreement on one precise point, that of political justice, that one expects that they will provide the force of a durable adhesion to the principles of justice. Besides, how can disagreements be reasonable if we take the professed beliefs to be mere prejudices or survivals of the past? We have to admit, with Thomas Nagel in his *Mortal Questions*,[12] that reason has its burdens,[13] precisely in the sphere of its practical and normative exercise, and with Isaiah Berlin that any system of institutions can only accept a limited number of founding values in its space of realization. Constitutional democracy therefore cannot economize on the "precepts of reasonable discussion,"[14] by which

---

11. "The Domain of the Political and Overlapping Consensus," *New York University Law Review* 64, no. 2 (1989): 236.

12. Cf. Thomas Nagel, *Mortal Questions* (New York: Cambridge University Press, 1979), 128–41.

13. Cf. "The Domain of the Political," 236–38.

14. Ibid., 238.

Rawls draws near to the Habermasian ethics of discussion, without renouncing his reticence as regards transcendental arguments. The idea of an overlapping consensus remains a pragmatic one, supported by at least two centuries of democratic practice. But even the idea of consensus has to be tempered by that of the expectation of support by a "substantial majority of its politically active citizens."[15]

Should Rawls be reproached for having misconstrued the problematic of domination which, in continental Europe at least, has largely occupied the scene of political philosophy from Hegel to Max Weber and Carl Schmidt? Rawls believes he has allowed for it with two important characteristics of the political relation: the closed character of a society we do not voluntarily enter or leave, and the coercive character of political power, if only as regards the application of laws.[16] Yet, if these two characteristics do belong to the delimitation of the "special domain of politics," they teach us nothing about the conditions of justice that will make a State a State of Right and a regime a constitutional regime. It is the adhesion of citizens as free and equal persons that justifies the general structure of political authority. The reasonable character of this adhesion consists in the fact that no community of religious, philosophical, or moral beliefs would take it as reasonable to make recourse to the power of the State in order to obtain the devotion of others to its particular doctrines.

Rawls reveals a bit more of his own estimation of the contemporary spiritual situation when he examines what he takes to be the typical case of an overlapping consensus. This is the one where the political conception is approved by the three following "comprehensive" doctrines: a religious conception that ties tolerance to its very self-understanding of its faith; a form of philosophical liberalism, like that of Kant or Mill, that derives the theory of justice as fairness as one of the consequences of its general vision of the world; and finally, a political conception sufficient by itself in its expression of its political values where "under the relatively favorable conditions that make a constitutional regime possible, that aim is a reasonable guide and may be in good part realized."[17] Rawls does not tell us where he

15. Ibid., 235.
16. Ibid., 242.
17. Ibid., 249.

situates himself as an individual in relation to this typical case of overlapping consensus. His role as a philosopher ends at the moment when he underscores the contingent character of the very conditions of stability without which the objection of *unreality* he addresses to the idea of a well-ordered society governed by the theory of justice as fairness, in the sense of *A Theory of Justice,* would remain insurmountable.[18]

18. See the Preface to *Justice et démocratie,* 9; *Political Liberalism,* xvii.

The Plurality of Instances of Justice

The theme of this lecture might appear inopportune, even untimely, in the precise sense of the word. At a time when public opinion and the public powers are questioning the nature of the transfers that our nation-state must yield to the present European institutions and those to come, and are asking if it is a question of a simple transfer of competence or a real transfer of sovereignty, which is reputed to be indivisible and, owing to this fact, inalienable—it is at this very time that I want to attempt to take the measure of a symmetrical problem, although one pointing in the opposite direction. Here it is no longer a question of a limitation from on high of what we can call the juridical power of the State, but of the limitation in a sense from below of this very juridical power. It is a question about a historical force, operating within a particular state, for which various authors are at work trying to formulate the theory. I propose examining two of these pleas in favor of an intrastate differentiation of generative instances of right. The first, that of Michael Walzer, in his *Spheres of Justice*,[1] has been taken as one of the most brilliant rebuttals yet offered of John Rawls and of his abstract, formal, and strictly procedural concept of justice. The second is that which Luc Boltanski and Laurent Thévenot present in their *De la justification: les économies de la grandeur.*[2] In this book, it is the idea of justification and not directly that of justice that provides the focus, while it is the cities and worlds governed by what the subtitle calls economies of scale or

1. Michael Walzer, *Spheres of Justice: A Defense of Pluralism and Equality* (New York: Basic Books, 1983).

2. Luc Boltanski and Laurent Thévenot, *De la justification: les économies de la grandeur* (Paris: Gallimard, 1991).

standing that introduce plurality at the very heart of the demand for justification. The target is no longer Rawls's procedural abstraction, but rather the apparent antinomy between the holism of Durkheimian sociologists and the methodological individualism professed by economic theory. It remains true, however, that these two works, despite their differences (which I shall discuss below), both deal with a pluralism that takes up—in an inverted fashion, so to speak—the unitary focus on the judicial that the nation-state constitutes in our Western and more precisely our republican tradition.

There is one pitfall I wish to avoid: that of a term-by-term comparison ending up with a mere juxtaposition of these two short monographs.

Beyond the difference in the way of dividing what are here called spheres and cities, I want to consider two questions. The first has to with the different nature of these projects and the criteria of distinction that result from this. The second, and more important, question, although governed by the first, concerns the new possibilities for regrouping the political community and its justice left open by these two enterprises of what we can call juridical pluralism. Indeed, if these two works invert our republican conception of the oneness of the source of juridicity, summed up by the concept of the sovereignty of the people, do they not invite us to take them in turn in an inverted manner by asking what there is to say, in the last analysis, about justice or justification as singular terms at the end of the long detour through multiplicity and the diversity of sources of right.

TWO PROJECTS OF PLURALIZATION

Approaching these two works beginning from the projects that set them on their way and the criteria of distinction that flow from these projects, we must first attend to the differences expressed in their subtitles: on the one side, "defense of pluralism and equality"; on the other, "the economies of *grandeur.*" What does this say?

Walzer's project has to do with equality. But the criterion of differentiation is provided by the notion of social goods. Thus it is necessary to examine the nature of this connection. Ever since Solon, Pericles, Isocrates, and Aristotle, equality has been a synonym of justice, once justice is held to govern the distribution of equal or unequal shares, in the varying senses I shall speak of as qualitative. Let us say that justice, in a distributive sense, identifies the idea of equality with that of a fair share. Difficulties begin when one sets aside simple equality—arithmetic equality, Aristotle said—following the formula, the same share to everyone. Only a repressive society, it is said, could impose such equality, and it would be to everyone's detriment. So what then of complex equality? The demand for such equality turns out to be essentially reactive or corrective, not to say abolitionist. What one wants to abolish is domination. Whence Walzer's project: "The aim of political egalitarianism is a society free from domination" (p. xiii). The same applies, as we shall see, for Boltanski and Thévenot. But how does domination manifest itself in our societies? Essentially in the way social goods are distributed. What can we do so that no social good serves as a means of domination? With this question we tie the project to its criterion, namely, the principle of differentiation of social goods. Three interconnected assertions serve as a guide here:

1. social goods are irreducibly multiple;

2. each one rests on some symbolism (Walzer calls it a shared understanding); and

3. each develops an internal logic, on the basis of the shared understanding of the groups in question, that is, the reasons that govern both the extent of its validity and the limit of the claim it makes.

These three assertions give us a threefold criterion for identifying the goods at issue, differentiating the implied symbolism in each case, and delimiting the concerned spheres.

Thus we can see how the project—to counteract domination—and the threefold criterion bound to the notion of social goods are articulated in terms of each other. The notion of complex equality then appears as the concept resulting from the intersection between the project of combating domination and the program of differentiating spheres of justice. Like the idea of simple equality, that of complex equality is a concept of protest, of abolition. From this, we can already presume that the concern for differentiation will win out over that of integration. But this will be the theme of the next section of this chapter.

If we now look at the open-ended list of social goods Walzer proposes, we are struck by several surprising features. My first impression is one of bric-a-brac—of *bricolage* in the sense made famous by Claude Lévi-Strauss. This effect is undeniably the one sought. If it is true that social goods are heterogeneous, the reasons that govern their evaluation are themselves incommensurable. A rapid glance at the list confirms this. We begin with membership. How is the inside and outside of a political community to be assigned between members and strangers? We continue with social provision, essentially security and assistance to those most in need, with the question what needs entail an obligation that they be provided for, along with a corresponding right to such provision? From there we pass on to money and commodities, with the question what can and cannot be bought with money? As complete a list as possible of what is not commercial answers this question. Therefore it is by considering the legitimate meanings attached to the notion of saleable goods that the limits attached to the notion of the market and to that of a market economy are decided. Next considered are offices open to rule-governed competitions, with a cluster of questions: What tests? Who judges? And above all: is every job to be considered an office? The whole question of a "right to" and the limits of the notion of public service in office are at issue here. This, curiously, is followed by the question of hard, degrading, or dangerous work, all taken to be negative values that need to be fairly distributed without regimenting the whole world. From here we pass to leisure activities, which, as positive, do not reduce to idleness, or vacations, but preside over the distribution of social time and the rhythms of activity in the city. It is not surprising next to read many pages devoted to education, which is a social good inasmuch as the transmission of knowledge and the formation of personal autonomy are traceable back to social symbolism. A string of questions touching on justice flows from the understanding of this good: Who teaches? To whom? Under the control of what offices? And above all, how to assure equality of opportunity, without falling once again into repressive systems through an excess of pedagogical zeal? The reader, educated in political philosophy, will be astonished to turn next to three chapters devoted to kinship and love, divine grace, and the struggle for recognition. This is another occasion to say that the list of social goods is long and open-ended, as soon as one takes into account the amplitude of shared symbolisms, the internal logic of the goods considered, and above all the delimitation that results from their spheres of validity. Who can deny that kinship, marriage, and the equality of the sexes pose questions of distribution? Or that the quarrel between Church and State calls for the curbing of rival pretensions, raised in turn by one side or the other across a line of demarcation bought at a high price? Finally, recognition itself is a social good in the form of titles, honors, compensations, and prizes, but also punishments:

> What we distribute to one another is esteem, not self-esteem; respect, not self-respect; defeat, not the sense of defeat; and the relation of the first to the second term in each of these pairs is indirect and uncertain. (p. 273)

We see that the notion of social goods extends far, even to the sphere of intimacy, and the problems of a just distribution pursue us to the very core of our conscience.

But we come to the last chapter, whose place in the whole edifice, or rather in its enumeration, will be at the center of our critical reflections when we come in the next section to ask ourselves about the resources for another grouping left open by one or the other of the juridical pluralisms we are considering. This last chapter is titled "Political Power." It is worth noting that in it we find no definition in the form of a State, even though we find enumerated (though not lingered over) sovereignty, authority, and the power of decision making. It is as one good among goods, therefore as a distributed good, that political power is sought and feared and resisted. If this is the case, it is because no other good poses in such a critical manner the problem of boundaries. Sometimes it is colonized by money, by the competence of experts, even by sex; sometimes it invades all the other spheres, to the point of giving tyranny its most visible form. How is it to be kept within its boundaries? Well, by proceeding as in the case of money, where it was asked what cannot be bought thanks to the internal logic of commercial goods. In the same way, one makes a list of what we cannot do with political power: tolerate slavery, corrupt the system of justice, discriminate among plaintiffs, control religion, confiscate or abusively tax property, arrogate to ourselves the monopoly of education, restrain basic liberties. For Walzer, this question about what political power can and cannot do precedes and commands the question of who governs. Taking up the much-used metaphor of the captain of the ship, he forthrightly proclaims that it is up the passengers, not the captain, to choose the destination and evaluate the risks. Here Walzer is close to Hannah Arendt, for whom power proceeds from the conjunction of wills and not from any higher agency.

In this regard, the most important peril for our societies comes from the coalition between property as power over things and political power as exercised over human beings. Whence the permanent urgency of a correct delimitation of spheres. Still the reader cannot fail to wonder: is political power a good like all the others? As the "crucial agency of distributive justice" (p. 281), is it not itself also the border guard? And, in this, does it not pose a quite specific problem of self-limitation, whether by constitutional or some other means? We touch here on what I shall call below the political paradox, namely that politics seems both to constitute one sphere of justice among others and to envelop all the other spheres.

Turning from Walzer to Boltanski and Thévenot, we are immediately struck by the difference not only at the level of their project but also in the criteriology that results from it. To the pair formed by the search for complex equality and the investigation of social goods corresponds another pairing: that between the search for justification and the investigation of orders of scale. These massive differences refer back to different initial situations. For Walzer, this is tyranny, the perverse form of domination; for Boltanski and Thévenot, it is conflict, disputes, differences of opinion, in short, discord. Domination calls for a curbing strategy, discord one of justification consisting of a battery of arguments intended to prevail in disputes or litigation. When so associated with the search for justification, the sense of injustice constitutes a motivation within the framework of disagreement no less strong than it does within that of domination. For it is violence that haunts discord once this fails to raise itself to the level of discourse. This then is the question from which this work proceeds: how to justify agreement and manage disagreement without succumbing to violence?

This project makes use of a methodology, or better a criteriology, consisting, as in the case of Walzer, of a work of differentiation. This is why an identical problem of redistribution will be considered below. However, differentiation does not bear here on social goods and shared understanding, but on principles of scale. The difference is not easy to make clear. Let us say that one starts by looking for forms of equivalence—and therefore generalities—among social actors, resulting from their recourse to final principles of legitimation in situations of agreement and disagreement. It is these principles that turn out in the end to be multiple.

It is necessary to stop somewhere in the regression toward always prior arguments. The necessity for such a halt in operations of justification cannot fail to interest the jurist reflecting on the relationship between judgment and stopping point: stop in deliberation, stop in the confrontation of claims, a final word pronounced in the debate of oneself with oneself or between oneself and another. But this is not all. We have not yet introduced the idea of scale or of an economy of scale. Orders of generality corresponding to forms of justification are not just a means of classification, but also scales of evaluation. Think of Pascal and his "established scales" [*grandeurs d'établissement*]—our authors have. That principles of justification govern relations of standing becomes obvious once the idea of justification takes over in determining what counts or does not count in qualifying tests.

Here is what for Boltanski and Thévenot occupies the place held for Walzer by the idea of a heterogeneity of social goods, namely, the plurality of principles of justification invoked when social actors undertake to plead for their cause or to uphold their criticism in situations of discord.

I do not want to push this opposition too far, for didactic reasons. There is a kinship between these two projects of pluralizing the idea of justice that brings them close together. We can show this by the implicit borrowings each makes from the other. For example, the notion of social goods develops an internal logical heavily freighted with a prescriptive load (for example, what one does or does not have the right to purchase). In this sense, the notion of a shared understanding links up with that of justification. In an opposite sense, we can say that scales of standing give rise to distributions just like that of social goods. Justification too then has to do with distributive justice. What is more, in both cases it is power, and therefore also satisfaction and enjoyment, that gets distributed. It is true, however, that the gap remains between a project aimed at equality, that is, at the limitation of domination, and one aimed at justification, that is, at a reasonable treatment of opposing claims.

This initial difference finds an echo on the plane of the models with which the two enterprises end up. It is not by chance that

Boltanski and Thévenot call into question not spheres of justice but cities and worlds. Regimes of justified action can be called "cities" insofar as they give some sufficient coherence to an order of human transactions. They are "worlds" insofar as some things—objects or arrangements—serve as established referents, something like a "common world," for tests that occur within a given city. Thus, in the "inspired" city, the standing of persons is authorized by grace or a gift, with no relation to money, glory, or utility. In the "city of opinion" standing depends on renown, on the opinion of others. In the "commercial" city, it is rare goods, submitted to everyone's envy, that are negotiated, people being united only through the agreement they find in their desires. In the "domestic" city, which extends to include what Hannah Arendt called the household, the values of loyalty, fidelity, and reverence reign. The "civic" city rests on the subordination of one's own interest to the will of the whole, expressed in positive law. In the "industrial" city, which is not to be confused with the commercial city where the instantaneous fixing of prices is what is operative, what dominates are long-standing functional rules submitted to the higher principle of utility.

The first striking thing is the superficial resemblance between these two works. The chapter on the commercial city recalls that on money and commodities; the civic city evokes political power; and one could easily find equivalencies between what is said on the one hand about the inspired city, and on the other about divine grace, or between the domestic city and free time, recognition, and so on. But we can doubt whether such a term-by-term correlation gets us very far, given that the methodology used differs so profoundly. Walzer draws on a cultural anthropology in the eyes of which the evaluation of social goods presents an enduring relative stability. In this, he proceeds as does Clifford Geertz in his "understanding of cultures." He confines himself to telling examples as a way of presenting the profiles of relatively stable and enduring evaluations. It is the idea of shared understandings that allows this procedure to work, which, after all, was already that of Max Weber with his elaboration of ideal types. Boltanski and Thévenot's cities are not ideal types of shared evaluations but rather forms of argumentation in situations of agreement and disagreement. This is why their reconstruction has to be more complex than a mere redoubling of the understandings effectively at work over a sufficiently long period. They consist curiously and, may I say, happily in a direct confrontation, with a view to clarifying them in terms of one another, of, on the one hand, speculative works received from the philosophical and theological tradition, and, on the other hand, training manuals intended for the managers of enterprises and for union leaders.

This intersecting reading is first put into practice in the setting of the commercial city. Our authors extract from Adam Smith the elements that assure the establishment of a commercial bond. These elements constitute, as Smith expresses it, the outlines of a "grammar" it is possible to identify in the weakest, least articulated of arguments, like those in the already mentioned training manuals. In the same way, Augustine's *City of God* is asked to bring to an appropriate level the weaker discourse articulated by spiritual guidebook authors, popular artists, and other marginal talents who people the inspired city. Rousseau's *Social Contract* is, as might be expected, the major resource for the civic city. Hobbes's conception of honor helps make explicit the subtle rules of hierarchy in the city of renown, where standing depends entirely on others' opinion. Saint-Simon is the guide for making use of the discourse of those he was the first to call industrialists. Bossuet and other moralists provide a discourse appropriate to the domestic city. (And I note in passing that philosophy finds itself reintroduced into the heart of the social sciences as an argumentative tradition, which constitutes both an indirect justification of it and, for our two authors, a sociologist and an economist, recognition of their belonging to a long history concerned with meaning.)

The advantage of the methodology at work in *De la justification* is to push much further the conceptual analysis that in Walzer is taken for granted, once the symbolism governing a category of social goods has been established. I want to show this in regard to two subdivisions where these two works seem to overlap: the commercial and the political bonds.

As regards the commercial bond, Walzer, who is essentially concerned to prevent one sphere from reaching into another, confines himself to a brief summary of what sharing, buying and selling, and exchanging can signify. He counts on a kind of clarifying intuition, applied to the internal logic of the goods under consideration, in order to make up his list of what cannot be bought or sold. In the end, it is by composing the list of items having to do with other categories of goods that one specifies, in a negative sort of way, the commercial good itself. In *De la justification,* a work of constitution based on a type of argumentation that is more evaluative of the commercial bond itself corresponds to this operation of marking things. We can even speak of a veritable constitution of a common good that leads individuals to surpass their singularity. I shall return in the next part to the role played by this notion of a common good, which our authors specify in each case in terms of the city under consideration. Thus, in the case of the commercial city, the common good is figured by the price that concludes the negotiation sparked off by the free play of desire for coveted things:

> The commercial bond unites persons through the intermediary of scarce goods open to the appetites of all and the competition of desires subordinates the price, attached to the possession of a good, to the desires of others. (p. 61)

It is clear therefore that it is the rules governing the market—rules, the authors say, similar to rules of grammar—that allow, secondarily, criticism of the pretension of the commercial sphere to contaminate all the other spheres. This example of the commercial city provides a good occasion for refining the difference between an evaluative approach and an argumentative one, whatever their undeniable kinship may be.

I would like now to consider the other register where the two analyses overlap: political power on the one hand, the civic city on the other. For Walzer, we have seen, the question of power touches closely on the major preoccupation of his book, namely, the fate of domination. We have equally seen that it is in discovering the list of what political power does not have the right to control that we outline the contours of the sphere of power. But this internal constitution is taken as already understood, whereas with Boltanski and Thévenot the social contract gives rise to a conceptual genesis, namely, the one that proceeds from the transference of sovereignty from the body of the king to the general will. This is the case of a kind of subordination where the common good is defined as a "public" good. Degrees of civic standing proceed from the reciprocal commitment between particular individuals and the general public, depending on whether the will that makes citizens act is singular or, on the contrary, turned toward the general interest. It is at this point that the analysis of the civic city leads to the same perplexities as does that of the sphere of political power. Is the civic city—the very oddness of this term ought already to alert us—a city like all others? Is its paradox not that it also envelops all the other cities? This perplexity will be at the center of the second part of this chapter.

But I want to say a few more words about the difference in strategy in these two books. This is all the more necessary once Boltanski and Thévenot complete their theory of "cities" with that of "worlds." Allow me to recall how our authors pass from the first to the second theme. The attention paid to the grammar that is constitutive of each city has to be accompanied (according to them) by attention to the ways in which the qualification of persons of this or that standing are tested. I will underline in passing the importance for jurists of the moment of judgment, which is the moment when a ruling that decides a dispute is given, ending any incertitude concerning the standing of the parties involved. What is important for our present analysis lies elsewhere, however. This is the use made of a basis in things, objects, states of affairs in those qualifying tests that authorize us to speak not just of cities but also of worlds. "From justice," say our authors, "the question of agreement thus leads to that of 'adjustment.'" (Thévenot has spoken more recently of what he calls "fitting action.") It is perhaps this attention to material states of affairs, comparable to the judicial apparatus of the tribunal, that most distances our authors from the phenomenology of shared symbolism and commits them instead to a criteriology of judgment under the heading of "tested judgment."[3] This is the part of Boltanski and Thévenot's work that runs the greatest risk of being overlooked. Yet it is here that our authors' approach is most clearly distinguished from that of Walzer. The passage from the idea of a city to that of a world allows, in effect, for verifying the grammar of works of political philosophy with the aid of forms of discourse that come closest to the actual practice of those training manuals destined for managers and union leaders, as guidebooks for real worlds. However, rather than prolonging this confrontation on the plane of the realization of these two projects which differ so in where they begin, let

3. For the kinship to judicial judgment, cf. ibid., 175–76.

us now turn toward the critical question posed at the beginning of this lecture.

TOWARD THE POLITICAL PARADOX

What resources for grouping the political body, and hence for unifying different foci of right, remain open when we come to the end of our reading of these books?

We cannot say that Walzer's book is completely lacking any encompassing aim. The theme of complex equality, a theme reckoned to be abolitionist and the polar opposite of domination, runs through every sphere. It is, if I may so put it, what holds everything together. This theme already appears in the subtitle, "a defense of plurality and equality." Let us understand this to mean pluralism at the service of complex equality. And let us recall the formula already quoted from *Spheres of Justice:* "The aim of political egalitarianism is a society free from domination" (p. xiii). With this theme, Walzer can enter into competition with Rawls at the level of Rawls's second principle of justice. More fundamentally, it is what authorizes preserving, in the very title of the book, the word "justice" in the singular. Everything that is subsequently said about domination stems from what we can call a minimal formalism, which is expressed in the working definitions of terms like monopoly, domination, dominance, or finally tyranny. This minimal formalism is further expressed in the correlation between the abolitionist project and the criteriology of social goods. In this respect, we can take as a formal feature the threefold criterion: heterogeneity of social goods, shared symbolism, and internal logic of the prescriptive import. But I want to emphasize a concept we have not yet considered, which is situated at the point of encounter between the project of differentiation and the criteriology drawn from the notion of social goods: the concept of *conversion,* and with it of *convertibility.* Conversion consists in the fact that a social good, let us say money, wealth, gets set up as a function of its value in another sphere of justice, say that of political power. Here is the ultimate secret of the phenomenon of dominance, defined as "a way of using social goods that isn't limited by their intrinsic meanings or that shapes those meanings in its own image" (pp. 10–11).

Conversion can thus be characterized as a kind of symbolic violence. For as Walzer states:

> A dominant good is converted into another good, into many others, in accordance with what often appears to be a natural process but is in fact magical, a kind of social alchemy. (p. 11)

This surprising text makes me think of the famous chapter in *Capital* devoted to the fetishism of merchandise, merchandise being given a kind of mystical grandeur thanks to a fusion of the economic and the religious. Walzer will refer to conversion a number of times, but leave it, without further reflection, its metaphorical status. But it is not nothing if we admit, with Walzer, that "we can characterize whole societies in terms of the patterns of conversion that are established within them" (ibid.). And again: "History reveals no single dominant good and no naturally dominant good, but only different kinds of magic and competing bands of magicians" (ibid.). Walzer's reticence to say more stems from the major stance in his book, which is vigilance over the frontiers, as though the concern to found or integrate the most far-reaching social bond blocked us from the task of combating monopolies and tyrannies, as though (but this is my personal interpretation) every foundational enterprise were condemned to play the perfidious magical game of conversion.

Yet can a theory exclusively concerned to differentiate spheres avoid the question of integration of these same spheres into a single political body? It is not that Walzer is unaware of this question. At the very moment he puts in place his argument, he declares, "the political community is the appropriate setting for this enterprise" (p. 28). But nowhere does the status of this setting become the object of a distinct reflection. This reticence explains certain anomalies in the treatment of the first and last spheres of justice: nationality and political power.

As regards the first sphere of justice, we must observe that all the other distributions of goods unfold within it. Nationality is not a social good like the others: "we don't distribute it among ourselves; it is already ours. We give it out to strangers" (p. 32). And again: "membership cannot be handed out by some external agency; its value depends upon an internal decision" (p. 29). In other words, here we run up against a phenomenon of self-constitution that is difficult to place under the aegis of distribution, except through the bias of a pairing:

citizen-foreigner. The unusual character of this phenomenon of self-constitution in relation to an idea of distributive justice is underscored again by the fact that almost all other social goods turn out to be goods that cross frontiers, for which the world constitutes the final distributive agency about which we say that it is "self-contained." In contrast, we have to say that "the political community is probably the closest we can come to a world of common meanings" (p. 28).

Reading the last chapter, which in a way corresponds in a polar manner to the first one, reinforces our difficulty. As I said at the end of the first section of this chapter, political power is both a shared good like the others and—if we are careful to watch over it—the guardian of the frontiers. But it soon becomes clear that what interests Walzer is not the status of popular sovereignty and its eventual indivisibility, hence the foundation of the political body, which would touch the very question of the source of right, but the likelihood of what has appeared to us as the major perversion of the process of evaluating goods, namely, the unwarranted conversion of one good into another: of wealth into political power, of political power into religious power, and so on. In this way the question of the unitary ground of the political body is avoided. At the same time, this work also avoids confronting the political paradox that is constituted by treating the State in terms of distributive justice. As a good to be distributed, political power has to be given its place among all other goods. This is a way of contributing to demystifying it. But, insofar as it is not just one good among others, insofar as it is what regulates different distributions, including those having to do with such incorporeal commodities as affective, mystical, and ethico-juridical goods, political power seems to overflow the framework of distributive justice and to pose the specific problem of its self-constitution and, correlative to this, of its self-limitation. Why does Walzer avoid posing the problem of the State and of sovereignty in terms of this paradox? Undoubtedly he would say that this problem has been dealt with so often that today it covers over the one that seems more urgent to him, the problem of a limited government. Thus his argument is not really with Rawls, on the point of the principles of justice, but with Nozick, on the point of minimal government. He is like the firefighter who runs to where the fire is—where there is a transgression of some frontier. And the peril is greatest in his eyes with the question of political power. Yet we may suspect that there is a more basic reason at work here. A political philosophy constructed entirely around the theme of the heterogeneity of social goods is poorly armed to pose the problem of the self-constitution of the political body along with the connected problems of its self-limitation.

So the question arises whether a theory of justification, concerned for its part to differentiate cities and worlds, is better prepared to confront this figure of the political paradox. As a first approximation, one could say that Boltanski and Thévenot's book is better prepared than is Walzer's to take up such all-encompassing considerations. Long analyses devoted successively to the "figures of criticism" in situations of disagreement, then to that particular form of a return to agreement constituted by a compromise, can be seen as responding to the theme of complex equality. This order of succession is important. We do not go directly to the possibilities of agreement on the scale of a unified political community. First we make a long detour through the conflict between different worlds. The two works certainly resemble each other in this way. From both sides, pluralism can lead to the beginning of a tragic vision of action, agreement in one city having as its price disagreement between cities. But what Walzer treats as a conflict between shared symbolic systems, in the extension of the heterogeneity of goods, Boltanski and Thévenot deal with as a conflict between principles of justification, hence as an exercise in criticism. The transfer from one world to another is characterized by a transfer of arguments capable of sapping from within the principles of scale of this or that city, submitted in this way to the fire of a suspicious judgment. This capacity for mutual challenges is structural and not accidental. The common good of one city is vulnerable to the critique provided by the vision of another common good that accounts for the common bond of another city. In this way, our authors are led to lay out the map of intersecting critiques leading from one world toward each of the five other worlds. I shall not go into detail here about the crossfire that results, wherein there are many missed shots. Instead I shall dwell upon one remark that will lead us directly to the question of compromise, where the overall significance of the work is finally at issue:

> There exists no overarching position, external to and above each of these worlds, from which the plurality of justices could be considered from on high, like a range of equally possible choices. (p. 285)

The absence of any overarching position is a major theme common to both these books. What is the result for a theory of compromise?

Does this offer new openings for a recomposition of a unitary idea of justice?

Let us first observe, as a kind of transition, that the critique exercised starting from one world toward others is carried out by people capable of changing worlds, and therefore of transporting with them the internal vision of the world from which they come. An implicit trickster theory is thereby presumed. It is the defector, the traitor, that allows our authors to write:

> The possibility of leaving the present situation and denouncing it by basing oneself on an external principle and, consequently, a plurality of worlds, constitutes therefore the condition for a justified action. (p. 289)

But is not this individual who goes over the wall, so to speak, moved by the vision of a common good that is not just that of one city, of one world?

This is the question that is finally at issue for this whole enterprise. And it is difficult to answer either yes or no to this question.

At the very beginning of the book, still at a very formal level—before we enter into the maze of cities, somewhat like when Walzer speaks of domination before beginning his tour of his spheres—our authors set out a series of axioms that directly anticipate the answer to our question. The first axiom is constituted by the principle of "the common humanity of all members of any city" (p. 96). This equalizes every human being as human, excluding in particular any slavery or any category of subhumans. But in the absence of any differentiation, this bond remains nonpolitical inasmuch as it only brings onstage a single man, an Adam. Eden is not a political setting. The perpetual agreement of all with all proposes nothing other than a utopia, at the limit of any city. It is only with the second axiom, the principle of dissimilarity, that at least two possible states for the members of a city can be distinguished. We are no longer in Eden. The tests that attribute different states of affairs can begin. Therefore only a model of humanity in different states gives access to a political life. This is why it is necessary to add a supplementary axiom that defines the model of a "well-ordered humanity" (p. 99). It is in terms of this polar status set over against the utopia of an undifferentiated Eden that we can talk about a common good, albeit in each case from the angle of some city or world.

Having made this reservation, we can return to the question of compromise, or rather compromises, between each city and the other five cities. All that ever exists are the figures of compromise. Thus it seems an improper use of the term when one of the last chapters is titled "Compromise for the Common Good" (p. 337). How can there be a supercompromise at the scale of the undivided political body, once compromise is only the suspension of some difference of opinion by which violence is avoided? That this is what is meant is clear:

> The principle intended by a compromise remains fragile so long as it cannot be referred back to a form of common good constitutive of a city. Putting in place a compromise does not allow ordering people in terms of some universal scale. (p. 338)

In reading the part of this book devoted to compromise, one gets the impression that compromises are always weaker than the internal bonds of the different cities. The result is that if some higher common good is affected by the compromise, as a general figure of interaction, it is just as indeterminate as the bond set up by the compromise is fragile. Outside the utopia of Eden there is only the possibility of dealing with disagreements in terms of compromises always threatened by turning into a compromising of principles, on a slippery slope that recalls the perverse effect denounced by Walzer under the heading of conversion.

I therefore want to ask whether, with Boltanski and Thévenot as with Walzer, one has not underestimated the paradox of the political, resulting from the fact that the civic city is not a city like all the others, in any case not in the sense that the market, the family, or the inspired city are. I see a reinforcement of my perplexity in the very choice these authors make of Rousseau's *Social Contract* as a model of the civic city. (And as regards the very term "civic city," our authors show some hesitation. Is it not a pleonasm?) If the *Social Contract* does work as a model, it is difficult to take it for the model of one city among others. It can only be the model of an inclusive city. To the extent that it is true that the general will tolerates no coalition within or outside itself, Rousseau would have called these other cities building "bricks."

Do these critical remarks undercut the analyses of Walzer and of Boltanski and Thévenot? I am more inclined to give credit to these two works for having helped us become aware of a previously unrecognized situation, or in any case one not thinkable in terms of our French republican and Jacobin tradition—that is, that the State, as the source of right, finds itself today placed in the uncomfortable situation of an entity called upon to behave at the same time as the whole and as the part, as the container and the contained, as an inclusive agency and an included region. It is in this sense that our authors' reticences, admitted or not, have become our own awkward position. This latter points to hard times for the question of rights. It will be no easier in the coming decades to reconcile indivisible popular sovereignty with the blossoming of a multitude of centers of rights than to reconcile this same indivisible sovereignty with new postnational, if not suprastate, institutions, which themselves will give rise to rights. Just as we shall have to deal with a complex situation, stemming from the intertwining of several agencies of juridicity at the level of the state and the suprastate, so too we shall more and more have to deal with a symmetrical situation issuing from the intertwining of several sources of juridicity at the infrastate level. This situation is a result of the figure that clothes the political paradox.

Aesthetic Judgment and Political Judgment According to Hannah Arendt

The goal of this essay is to examine Hannah Arendt's thesis, presented in the third—unfortunately unfinished and posthumously published—volume of her trilogy *Thinking, Willing, Judging*,[1] the thesis that it would be possible to extract from the Kantian corpus, under the heading of the philosophy of history, a theory of *political judgment* that would satisfy the criteria applied to aesthetic judgment in the third Critique, the *Critique of Judgment*.

AESTHETIC JUDGMENT: KANT

Before taking up Arendt's hypotheses it will be useful to recall briefly the analyses Kant devotes to reflective judgment, of which aesthetic judgment is one of two expressions, putting the accent on their capacity to be extrapolated beyond the field covered by the third *Critique*. If I do not begin straightaway with his analysis of aesthetic judgment and linger over the encompassing concept of reflective judgment, it is so that I may leave a place for an alternative interpretation of Kant's political philosophy, one that will remain under the aegis of reflective judgment but not exclusively in terms of its aes-

---

1. The three volumes were to have been titled *The Life of the Mind*. Of the third volume, we have only her *Lectures on Kant's Political Philosophy* along with a seminar on *The Critique of Judgment* and an essay by Ronald Beiner (Chicago: University of Chicago Press, 1982). Myriam Revault d'Allonnes has translated the *Lectures* (along with the Postscript to volume I of the *Life of the Mind*) into French under the title *Juger. Sur la philosophie politique de Kant* (Paris: Seuil, 1991). Along with Beiner's essay, she adds one of her own, titled "Le courage de juger."

thetic use. I shall begin therefore from the junction of the aesthetic and the teleological judgment, under the encompassing concept of reflective judgment.

Let me say first of all that this conjunction demands a profound reworking of the very conception of judgment. The whole philosophical tradition up to Kant rested on the logical definition of judgment as a predicative act (to give a predicate to a subject). The fundamental reversal Kant brought about consists in substituting for the idea of attribution (or predication) that of subsumption, that is, an act by which a case is "placed under" a rule. The great innovation of the third *Critique* in relation to the first *Critique* is that it allows for a split within the idea of subsumption. In the first *Critique,* subsumption proceeds so to speak from above to below, from the rule toward the fact of experience. This is the determinative judgment, so called because, in the application of a rule to a case, this judgment confers on experience the truth value of objectivity (without any reference to the idea of adequation to the thing in itself = X). The *Critique of Judgment* presents the hypothesis of an inverse functioning of subsumption. For a given case, one "seeks" the appropriate rule under which to place the singular experience. This judgment is "merely" reflective because the transcendental subject does not determine any universally valid objectivity, but instead only takes into account the procedures the mind follows in the operation of subsumption, proceeding in a way from below to above.[2] It is this amplitude of the notion of reflective judgment that we must keep in mind in the following discussion. Nonetheless, we cannot pass over in silence the priority Kant himself gives to aesthetic judgment in relation to teleological judgment. This priority results from the fact that the natural order thought in terms of the idea of finality itself has an *aesthetic* dimension in virtue of its very relation to the subject and not to the object. Order affects us in that it pleases us. With this, aesthetic judgment is called for by teleological judgment as the first component of reflective judgment, hence as regards pure reflection. Already in section VII of the "Introduction," Kant can write that the object is said to be beautiful and that the power of judging on the basis of such pleasure (and consequently in a universally valid manner)

2. Immanuel Kant, *Critique of Judgment,* trans. Werner S. Pluhar (Indianapolis: Hackett, 1987), 18–19 (Ak, V, 179).

is called taste. This cannot be said of mechanical order. It is not pleasing, for it does not respond to any expectation (*Absicht*) capable of being disappointed or fulfilled. It seems legitimate therefore to place the judgment of taste at the head of an investigation that seems first destined to find its full blossoming in a reflection on the natural finality presented by living organisms. The fragile unity of the two parts of the third Critique rests finally on this possibility of shifting the accent, either to the *pleasure* of order or to its *teleological* structure. The transcendental aesthetic, left to itself, would face the threat of falling back into psychologism; transcendental teleology into naturalism. What assures a certain primacy to the judgment of taste in relation to the teleological judgment is the more immediately recognizable kinship between the beautiful and our expectation of a pure pleasure.

Having said this, two features of the *judgment of taste* will draw our attention: first, that taste should be a *judgment,* next that it is its *communicability* alone that assures its universality. These two features constitute the two major axes of the "Analytic of the Beautiful" (which we shall see below is completed by an "Analytic of the Sublime").

In the first place, it is surprising that a more intimate sense than seeing or hearing, namely, taste (*Geschmack*), should be the support of a judgment. Following Gracian, Kant begins by emphasizing its immediately discriminating character (that is, that it is capable of distinguishing the beautiful from the ugly), then its attachment to the particular, and finally its capacity for reflection. About what does taste reflect? About the free play among the representative faculties, essentially of the imagination (and its spontaneous character) and the understanding (as a function of order). The aesthetic pleasure that results from this reflection on free play is pure pleasure. It is pure pleasure in that, first of all, the judgment of taste does not make us know anything about the object, either in itself or as a cognitive phenomenon. What is more, this pure pleasure equally escapes moral censure precisely inasmuch as its attachment to the free play of imagination and understanding assures its disinterested character. The reflective aspect of this judgment has to do wholly with its referring not to a property of the beautiful thing, but to the state of free play of the representative faculties. In order to underscore the oddness of this "qualitative" moment, Kant risks two paradoxes that have fascinated his interpreters. The first is the paradox of something that *pleases without a concept*, that is, without any objectifying intention and without any claim to truth. This paradox is explained by the opposition between an objectifying, hence conceptual intention and a reflective intention applied solely to the free play of imagination and understanding. This first paradox lends itself to the kind of transposition outside the aesthetic field attempted by Hannah Arendt. Let us therefore retain this idea of a free play whose two poles are the understanding (that is, an ordering function) and the imagination (that is, a function of invention, creativity, fantasy).

The second paradox by means of which Kant underscores the strangeness of the pleasure included in the judgment of taste is the idea of a *finality with no end* indicated in the title of the "third moment" of the Analytic of the Beautiful (§10). Here finality means an internal composition such that the parts are mutually adjusted to one another and to the whole. It is the finality that one finds elsewhere in the organization of living beings dealt with in the second part of the *Critique of Judgment*. But it is also a finality without an end in the sense that it is not sought or projected, as is the case in the relation between means and end in the techniques constitutive of human praxis. A beautiful flower presents this harmonious composition without referring back to some intentional activity.

Next it is unexpected that the judgment of taste claims universality. Hasn't this been endlessly discussed? The solution: taste is capable of a quite original form of universality, namely, communicability. Taste is a shared sense. And what is shared is precisely the reflection on the free play of the representative faculties. Taste therefore is universalizable in another way than are objective representations or the practical maxims of the free will. This equation between universality and communicability is without precedent in the first two Critiques. We need to acknowledge the paradox of such communicability. It is a true paradox in the sense that nothing seems more incommunicable than a pure pleasure. Yet, to the extent that it is due to the contemplation of an inner finality, that is, to the mutual fittingness instituted by the free play of the faculties, this pleasure is in principle capable of being shared, ideally, by everyone. To reckon something beautiful is to admit that this thing "must also involve a claim to being valid for everyone" (§6 is titled, "The Beautiful Is What Is Presented without Concepts as the Object of a *Universal* Liking"). To detach universality from objectivity, then reattach it to what pleases without concepts and, what is more, is about something that presents the form of final-ity without the requirement of being treated like the means to some projected and sought-for end constitutes an extremely audacious ad-vance in the question of universality, as soon as communicability does not result from some antecedent universality. It is this paradox of communicability, as instituting universality, we are tempted to seek in other domains than aesthetics (in particular in the political domain, but also in that of history or eventually of the juridical).

In the "Analytic of the Beautiful" Kant only explores the more easily graspable implications. For example, the exemplarity of the beautiful inasmuch as it calls for something following (*Nachfolge*) that would not be an imitation (*Nachahmung*) except at the price of ceasing to be a judgment, that is, a critical discernment. Such a dis-tinction between following and imitating opens the way to broad considerations on the dialectic between tradition and innovation.

That Kant here bases himself on the well-known *topos* of "com-mon sense" should not distract us, for his whole effort consists in dis-tinguishing this common sense from an empirical consensus (which would be precisely the sociological effect of a servile imitation). The "fourth moment" of the "Analytic of the Beautiful," devoted to the "modality" of the judgment of taste, bears precisely on the kind of necessity that is attached to this universal communicability of the feeling of the beautiful. (In the first part of Hans-Georg Gadamer's *Truth and Method* there is a long analysis of the tradition of "com-mon sense," so open to misunderstanding and misreading, but also so difficult to state in the right terms; for example, in the vocabulary of exemplarity, wherein historicity and perenniality intersect.)[3]

I have said nothing here about the Analytic of the Sublime Kant added to his analytic of the beautiful. Far from weakening the para-doxes of what pleases without concepts and of a finality without end, the sublime heightens them. Kant wanted here to account for the two different functions of the play of the imagination and the un-derstanding: a harmonious, proportioned, calming play and a dis-cordant, disproportional one, whose excess gives rise to a surplus of thought. This dialectic of the judicatory imaginary will also have parallels outside aesthetics. In distending the play of imagination

---

3. Hans-Georg Gadamer, *Truth and Method*, 2d rev. ed., trans. revised by Joel Wein-shiemer and Donald G. Marshall (New York: Crossroads, 1991).

and understanding, or let us say of fantasy and order, nearly to the breaking point, the sublime opens the space into which can be inserted some of the procedures that contribute to the construction of the reflective judgment in other fields than the aesthetic. The sublime, in turn, can take on two forms: in the "mathematical" sublime our imagination outruns, overflows, gets caught up in what is "absolutely grand," that is, beyond comparison. The faculty of judging then applies without measuring it to what is properly *immeasurable.* The work of the imagination, in failing in a progression to infinity to equalize itself with the overwhelming grandeur of the sublime, will find noteworthy equivalents in other areas than the aesthetic one, in particular in the negative sublime of the monstrous events of history. As for the "dynamic" sublime, it stems from the inadequacy of our forces compared to those of a nature that would crush us if we were not sheltered from its blows. This lack of measure too will find parallels elsewhere than in aesthetics. It is true that Kant was not interested in these possibilities of extrapolation so much as in the opening from aesthetics to ethics assured by the sublime. In effect, it is our superiority as moral beings that the aesthetic sublime helps to make manifest. We shall not follow Kant down this path by which the aesthetic points in the direction of the ethical. Rather, it is the work of an imagination invited to "think more" that shall hold our attention.

We should not limit the critique of aesthetic judgment to the "Analytic of the Beautiful," not even as augmented by that of the sublime. We need also to take into account the "Dialectic of Genius and Taste," which culminates in §48. So far we have been able to speak of the beautiful without specifying whether the judgment of taste bears on a product of nature ("this rose is beautiful") or a work created by a human artist. Kant seeks to delay the moment of "making" in order to avoid having an external finality interfere with the finality without end of the beautiful as such. This is why the primacy of nature is reaffirmed at the very heart of his investigation of the fine arts. In §45 he states that "Fine art is an art insofar as it seems at the same time to be nature." In effect, the finality visible in the products of fine art should not appear to be intentional, even though it is. Still, what is signified by this title at first seems surprising. Artistic beauty is subordinated to natural beauty a second time by the thesis that the genius from which the work of art proceeds is born of nature: "Genius is the talent (natural endowment) that gives the rule to art" (§46).

This does not prevent genius and taste from being opposed to each other, in this way placing a limit on any concern to subordinate art to nature. Kant goes as far as possible with this opposition. Just as taste reflects after the fact, so too genius invents without rules, in a way outrunning itself. The creative function, the source of originality, is opposed to the discriminating function of taste. And if great works are exemplary, their exemplarity, more than that of nature, is quite the contrary of servile and repetitive imitation. Here the opposition between "following" and "imitating" takes on its full meaning. We must then grant that *"judging* beautiful objects to be such requires *taste;* but fine art itself, i.e., *production* of such objects, requires *genius."* Is genius then not at the expense of taste? Yes, to a point: "taste is merely an ability to judge, not to produce" (§48). With great effort it seems, Kant assures the equal play of genius and taste:

> Taste, like the power of judgment in general, consists in disciplining (or training) genius. It severely clips its wings, and makes it civilized or polished: but at the same time it gives it guidance as to how far and over what it may spread while still remaining purposive. It introduces clarity and order into a wealth of thought, and hence makes the ideas durable, fit for approval that is both lasting and universal, and [hence] fit for being followed by others and fit for an ever advancing culture. (§50)

This competition between taste and genius will be of the greatest importance for us when we transpose it to the plane of political judgment. It will become, in the hands of Hannah Arendt, the competition between a cosmopolitan spectator and the agent of history. A question similar to that posed by the confrontation between taste and genius will then spring up in the political field. Does not the last word fall to the disinterested spectator of great events, events that, however, only get inserted into history thanks to an exemplarity comparable to that of genius?

FROM AESTHETIC TO POLITICAL JUDGMENT:
HANNAH ARENDT

Hannah Arendt's effort in her volume on Judging—which we must not forget was left unfinished—can first be understood as a wager, namely, that it is finally more profitable to attempt to disengage a conception of political judgment from the theory of the judgment of taste than to bind this conception to the theory of teleological judgment *via* a philosophy of history. This is a large wager because the ties between the philosophy of history and the teleological judgment are more immediately perceptible in Kant's work, if only because Kant did write out his philosophy of history, whereas the political philosophy Hannah Arendt attributes to him is in large part a reconstruction, even if it remains inchoate, even virtual.

The interest a text like Kant's *Idea for a Universal History from a Cosmopolitan Point of View* (1784) continues to hold lies in the fact that, however marked by a natural teleology it may be, this philosophy of history is meant precisely to set in place a political philosophy.[4] It is true that this political philosophy is not a philosophy of political judgment. It is limited to articulating the political *task* assigned to the human species as regards natural finality, that is, as regards the innermost dispositions of this species. The very expression "a cosmopolitan point of view" expresses the singularity of this hinge point. The nine theses of the essay are meant to establish, degree by degree, the conditions of possibility of the transition from natural teleology to world citizenship—from *cosmos* to *polis*, we might say. The main turning point in the essay is found in theses five, six, and seven, where Kant affirms that it is by means of the "unsociable sociability" that governs the relations of an unenlightened humanity that nature exercises its pressure on the human species, which it leaves for all that entirely helpless. In these theses that develop the properly political dimension of the essay, the constitution of a civil society "administering the law in a universal fashion" is presented not as a gift of nature but as a task, more precisely as a "problem" that must be resolved. Nature does not propose the solution, but imposes both a problem and the impulse to resolve it. We can thus understand why this problem should be said to be "the most difficult and the last to be solved by mankind" (thesis 6). So while it is indeed nature that "disposes" humanity toward a cosmopolitan order, it is up to human beings to carry this task to a satisfactory completion.

In my opinion, there are three reasons why the outline of a phi-

---

4. Immanuel Kant, *Idea for a Universal History from a Cosmopolitan Point of View*, in *Kant On History*, ed. Lewis White Beck (Indianapolis: Bobbs-Merrill, 1963), 11–26.

losophy of political judgment such as Hannah Arendt proposes as an extension of aesthetic judgment cannot be dissociated from the explicit philosophy of history, whose leading moments we have just recalled. First, the 1784 essay can already be advantageously placed under the sign of reflective judgment, despite its appearance almost ten years before the *Critique of Judgment.* Is not the concept of a "perfect civil constitution," to which the seventh thesis is devoted, projected as an Idea *under* which the empirical signs of a promising development of the human species can be subsumed? In this regard, the ninth thesis is highly instructive: "It is strange and apparently silly to wish to write a history in accordance with an Idea of how the course of the world must be if it is to lead to certain rational ends. It seems that with such an idea only a novel could be written." But why not a novel, that is, a narrative? It is in Kant's series of responses to this suspicion that I see what I propose calling the place marker for a still unthematized reflective judgment. The first reason is that Kant says:

> If one may assume that Nature, even in the play of human freedom, works not without plan or purpose, this Idea could still be of use. Even if we are too blind to see the secret mechanism of its workings, this Idea may still serve as a guiding thread for presenting as a system, at least in broad outlines, what would otherwise be a planless conglomeration of human actions.

An Idea, serving as a guideline in the passage from conglomeration to system—is this not related to the nature of a reflective judgment? Not some fantastic dream, nor a transcendental imperative, but a directive Idea. Whence my suggestion that the *political* judgment Hannah Arendt spells out would not be the only extrapolation possible from the critical theory of reflective judgment. My second reason: the Idea serving as a guideline to the cosmopolitan point of view on history has as backing only the signs, symptoms, and indications that nourish the "hope finally that after many reformative revolutions, a universal cosmopolitan condition, which Nature has as her ultimate purpose, will come into being as the womb wherein all the original capacities of the human race can develop" (eighth thesis).

Is it not this same constellation of positive signs that political judgment will gather together, according to the analysis Hannah Arendt will make of it? A final reason: the note of hope Kant's essay of 1784 ends with is not foreign to what we can call political judgment; rather, it is consubstantial with it, to the extent that, as we shall see, political judgment cannot be limited to retrospection but includes a prospective, even prophetic dimension.

If, in her attempt to reconstruct a philosophy of political judgment, Hannah Arendt believed she could circumvent the philosophy of history, it was because this latter has for its subject not individual citizens, but the human species taken as a whole, as is indicated in the first thesis of Kant's 1784 essay. There is another reason: while we might take Kant's philosophy of history as having been eclipsed by those of Vico, Hegel, or Marx, his presumed philosophy of political judgment would not be threatened by a similar disaffection. What is more, it would be the promise of a critical, nonspeculative philosophy of history, one that would call for consideration of fragmentary histories closely tied up with political judgment. In this respect, Hannah Arendt could legitimately be suspicious that a philosophy of history that remained tributary to a philosophy of nature and that was deliberately oriented toward the future of the human species would block off an interest turned toward politics as such, that is, as distinct from mere sociability.

This said, the first theme of such a political philosophy will be the *plurality* implied in the willingness to live together that underlies politics. This condition of plurality offers an evident kinship with the requirement of *communicability* implied by the judgment of taste. Not only does this concept stemming from the third Critique receive a decisive clarification from its use within the framework of political judgment, it offers in return the means for a political reinterpretation of the judgment of taste. We recall the paradox: how to understand that taste, a more intimate sense that sight or hearing, should be understood as eminently communicable as the internal discernment of pleasure? In fact, what assured the transition from the intimate subjectivity of taste to the communicability that assures its universality was common sense. Thus we can ask whether this latter does not have, if not essentially, at least in terms of its destination, a political aspect, namely, to be both the condition and the effect of the life in common that is constitutive of a political body. Hannah Arendt goes so far as to distinguish the Latin usage of *sensus communis* from the popular notion of common sense as a given sociological fact. Certainly, the *sensus communis* is a sense of community that common people share with no need of help from philosophers. But its status as a required condition distinguishes it from any empirical fact.

The second theme will be that of the *particularity* of political judgment, comparable to that of aesthetic judgment ("*this* rose is beautiful"). Understood in this way, political judgment aims not at suppressing, but rather at justifying the particularity of historical events. Yet rather than nondescript, this particularity is exemplary. This feature—*the exemplarity of the particular*—is common to both the judgment of taste and historical judgment. And herein lies the justification of the concept we have already referred to of the *sensus communis*. What the *sensus communis* distinguishes and acknowledges is the exemplarity of the particular. In this regard, the comparison between the exemplarity of great events that give or allow for hope and that of beautiful things or works provides a new handhold for a philosophy of political judgment freed more than ever from the tutelage of a natural finality. It is in light of this theme of exemplarity that we can recognize the indicative, symptomatic value of events such as the French Revolution.

Further, we need to underscore the primacy of the retrospective view of the *spectator* over the prospective view of the *actors* of history. In this way we rediscover the opposition already encountered on the aesthetic plane between taste and genius, between the discernment of the one and the creativity of the other. It is for such a spectator that the significance of certain remarkable events of the past engenders a seed of hope, over against the melancholy a nonreflective sentiment might nourish. In this regard, the apparent contradiction one might see in Kant's different evaluations of the French Revolution finds its solution. For example, in *The Conflict of the Faculties* (Part 2, §5), Kant writes:

> There must be some experience in the human race which, as an event, points to the disposition and capacity of the human race to be the cause of its own advance toward the better, and (since this should be the act of a being endowed with freedom) toward the human race as being the author of this advance. But from a given cause an event as an effect can be predicted [only] if the circumstances prevail which contribute to it.[5]

5. Immanuel Kant, *The Conflict of the Faculties*, trans. Mary J. Gregor (Lincoln: University of Nebraska Press, 1992), 151.

Yet what is most important is that it is for retrospection, and for a spectator not engaged in the production of the event, that these circumstances—here the French Revolution—take on meaning:

> It is simply the mode of thinking of the spectators which reveals itself *publicly* in this game of great revolutions, and manifests such a universal yet disinterested sympathy for the players on one side against those on the other, even at the risk that this partiality could become very disadvantageous for them if discovered. Owing to this universality, this mode of thinking demonstrates a character of the human race at large and all at once; owing to its disinterestedness, a moral character of humanity, at least in its predisposition, a character which not only permits people to hope for progress toward the better, but is already itself progress in so far as its capacity is sufficient for the present. (§6, p. 153)

Despite the Terror, this revolution

> nonetheless finds in the hearts of all spectators (who are not engaged in this game themselves) a wishful participation that borders closely on enthusiasm, the very expression of which is fraught with danger; this sympathy, therefore, can have no other cause than a moral predisposition in the human race. (Ibid.)

As we can see, this text from 1798 does not dissociate political judgment from the cosmopolitan point of view of the 1784 essay.

So, disinterestedness, after the factness, and communicability constitute features that go hand in hand. If these features of the judgment of taste can be extended in a convincing way from aesthetics to politics, it is because they are tied to the reflective judgment in all its possible applications. Already, on the plane of the judgment of taste, the public use of critical thought expresses Judging in terms of its greatest generality. Section 40 of the *Critique of Judgment* speaks of universal (or general) communicability. And this communicability is expressed in conjunction with an "operation of reflection."

All these features are summed up in the lovely phrase "a broadened way of thinking" proposed in §40 of the *Critique of Judgment*. This broadening projects the critical perspective beyond sociological proximity and turns it toward other possible judgments, once the imagination invites us to "think from the standpoint of everyone else," recalling the expression referred to earlier. We may subsequently concern ourselves with the dangers of an aestheticization of

the political. Still we must do justice to the happy discovery thanks
to which the Aesthetic sees itself in turn elevated to the political
point of view and—why not?—to a cosmopolitical point of view.
Indeed, to the extent that the Kantian world citizen is, as Hannah
Arendt says, in fact a *Weltbetrachter*, a world spectator, it is the detached regard of this spectator that opens the way of hope to the de-
spairing witnesses of the horrors of history.

We can, nevertheless, oppose two series of reservations to this
remarkable reconstruction. The first have to do with the excessive disjunction made between the prospective orientation of the teleological judgment belonging to a text like the *Idea for a Universal History
from a Cosmopolitan Point of View* and the retrospective judgment of
the spectator on the aesthetic and political plane. The acknowledged
exemplarity of works of art, like that of great historical events, would
not constitute a pledge of hope if exemplarity did not serve as a handhold, if not a proof, for hope. How apart from some underlying teleology can the regard directed to the past turn back in expectation
toward the future? Hope, for Kant, appears as a bridge between the
regard of the witness and the expectation of the prophet. We recall
the final sentence of the Eighth thesis of the *Idea for a Universal History* evoking the "hope finally that . . . a universal cosmopolitan condition . . . will come into being." This link between retrospection and
hope is also stated in almost identical terms in the text from the *Conflict of the Faculties* already cited. In 1798, it was indeed again a question
of "the prophetic history of the human race": "There must be some
experience in the human race which, as an event, points to the disposition and capacity of the human race to be the cause of its own advance toward the better. . . . " The concept of *disposition* continues to
join the teleological and cosmopolitan points of view. Through it,
teleological and aesthetic judgment ally their paradigms in the project of a political philosophy said to have been left unwritten. Without this conjunction, could Kant have said of the French Revolution:
"For such a phenomenon in human history *is not to be forgotten*" (*Conflict of the Faculties,* §7, p. 159). This paragraph 7 is titled precisely
"Prophetic History of Humanity." The retrospective signs for reflective judgment are prospective as regards those projections authorized
by the "disposition" with which nature has endowed human beings as
destined to strive for a cosmopolitan state. These remarks attenuate
without suppressing the paradox of the distance between the specta-

tor's point of view and that of the moralist of action which we can call antirevolutionary. Nothing however says that the judgment of the spectator irremediably condemns the practical initiative of the revolutionary. Just as taste would have nothing to judge without the creative genius, the spectator of the Revolution would have nothing to admire without the audacity of the revolutionary.

Hegel will claim to resolve this paradox in the well-known passage devoted to the "pardon" the man of action and the beautiful soul exercise with regard to each other, which concludes chapter 6 of the *Phenomenology of Spirit.* It seems, however, if a passageway can be perceived in Kant between the two points of view, as though we should look for it on the side of the role attributed to "educated opinion," the only political public competent in Kant's eyes, inasmuch as it is subject both to the retrospective judgment directed to history that has occurred *and* to the hope founded on the "disposition" received from the hands of nature. Otherwise, one cannot see how the enthusiasm of the spectator could be incorporated into the prudent and moderate anticipation of a definitive progress of humanity. Only educated opinion is capable of joining, in the perception of events, the meaning we can assign to reflective judgment *and* the value of the sign, of the symptom, hope draws upon when it turns from retrospection to expectation.

A second line of criticism would run as follows. Is not the required place for active and prospective citizens, as in a text like *Perpetual Peace* (1795), better defined by the "Doctrine of Right" (1796) than by an extrapolation from the judgment of taste? *Perpetual Peace* provides the occasion for a reflection on war parallel to that we have seen concerning the French Revolution. War, too, receives two different interpretations: for the spectator and for the actor. For the former it is the midwife of meaning, even while it is absolutely condemnable as a *project* that can only be addressed to the actors of current history. As a ruse of nature, war is accessible and, it seems, tolerable only to the regard of a spectator. At the same time, as an enterprise submitted to moral judgment, it is intolerable and absolutely condemnable. In *Perpetual Peace,* war is what ought not to happen: "No state shall by force interfere with the constitution or government of another state."[6] What follows here from the "final

6. Immanuel Kant, *Perpetual Peace,* in *Kant On History,* Section I, §5, 89.

design" of nature, namely, the inauguration of a cosmopolitan unity, is a properly juridical obligation, and the events celebrated by political judgment take place as the articulation of this design of nature and this veto of practical reason.

We must not therefore hypostatize the judgment of the spectator, even if it is given to this spectator to embrace the scene as a whole, as does, after all, the philosophy of universal history. All that we can suggest is that reflection, in bearing on past events, reveals its prospective dimension thanks to a critical distancing. We must not therefore bind together in a univocal fashion reflection and retrospection. Otherwise, how will past events be able to appear as filled with promises, hence filled with the future?

In my opinion it is in the Doctrine of Right, dealt with rather too severely by Hannah Arendt, that we will find fruitful suggestions concerning the tie between retrospection and prospection, inasmuch as the "Doctrine of Right" lies at the turning point between the view of citizenship and that cosmopolitan point of view, stemming from a philosophy of history. This is due to the projective power of its requirements concerning the law-governed State and peace among such States. The philosophy of right then needs to be placed in an intermediary position between those "dispositions" arising from a natural finality and the *moral* requirement of a law-governed State, both in cities and among cities. We cannot place the whole weight of this demand on reflective judgment.

What can, perhaps, be retained in favor of Hannah Arendt's interpretation is that reflective judgment prevents the Kantian philosophy of history from tipping over into a philosophy of a Hegelian type in which Spirit takes over for nature, and where the cunning of reason would replace that of nature. Short of this decisive step, where Spirit itself gets substituted for the human species in the position of the subject of history, the world citizen remains, as Hannah Arendt puts it, a world spectator, and reflective judgment remains unreconciled with the rule of practical reason—at least so long as we neglect the mediation of the "Doctrine of Right." The sole indication of such reconciliation for a *critical* philosophy is the exemplarity that gives a point of futurity to communicability and, in this way, a "prophetic" dimension to reflective judgment itself.

Interpretation and / or Argumentation

This study stems from a lecture given in a seminar at the Ecole nationale de la magistrature under the apparently unequivocal title of "interpretation." What I propose here, under my double title, is an analysis where interpretation is paired with a presumably rival operation, namely, argumentation. What might justify this polarization where the first effect is to complicate the issue, at the moment when philosophers and jurists, moralists and magistrates are trying to elaborate a unified conception of the argument?—I mean that phase of a trial which I have shown above unfolds between the moment of uncertainty characteristic of the opening of the trial and the moment of pronouncing the verdict where this initial uncertainty is ended by a speech act that states the law. Therefore it is the epistemological coherence of such argument, in the judicial sense of the term, that is at issue here. It is a prior question whether, given the broad sense in which the notion of interpretation was used in this seminar, taken as a synonym for application (application of the juridical norm to a case in litigation), we can assign to this notion a more restricted connotation that justifies our opposing to it, at least as a first approximation, that of argumentation. The question is relevant insofar as argument has been characterized, among other things, as a verbal battle without violence and, more precisely, as the clash of arguments, by which the well-known agonistic tenor of arguments within the setting of a court of justice is underscored. The major question, then, is whether we must cling to a purely antinomial conception of the polarity of interpretation and argumentation or whether, as I believe, we must attempt to elaborate a properly dialectical version of this polarity.

In fact, the present state of the discussion does not seem, at first sight, oriented toward such a dialectical treatment. Our readings in the seminar mentioned dealt with, on the one side, an author like Ronald Dworkin, who places the whole second part of his work *A Matter of Principle* under the title "Law as Interpretation," apparently without making any place made for an eventual confrontation between interpretation and argumentation.[1] On the other side, we encountered theoreticians of juridical argumentation, like Robert Alexy[2] and Manuel Atienza,[3] for whom juridical argumentation must be considered as a distinct province, yes, but a subordinate one, within a general theory of practical argumentation, without interpretation ever being recognized as an original component of juridical discourse (*Diskurs*).

Despite this factual situation, which we shall unfold at our leisure, I thought I could draw an argument from the internal insufficiencies of each of the positions considered that would support my thesis that a juridical hermeneutic centered on the thematic of argument requires a dialectical conception of the relations between interpretation and argumentation. I was encouraged in this undertaking by the analogy that seemed to me to exist, on the epistemological plane, between the pair "interpret" and "argue" and, on the juridical plane, between "understand" and "explain," whose dialectical structure I have previously demonstrated with regard to the theory of the text, the theory of action, and the theory of history.

DWORKIN: FROM INTERPRETATION TO ARGUMENTATION?

In Dworkin's presentation of his ideas on this subject, I would place the accent on what I will gladly call the strategic framing within which appeal is made to the notion of interpretation, with the confessed goal of seeking the inherent limits of this framework, the reasons for overshadowing the problematic of argumentation that, for

---

1. Ronald Dworkin, *A Matter of Principle* (Cambridge: Harvard University Press, 1985).

2. Robert Alexy, *Theorie des juristischen Argumentation* (Frankfurt: Suhrkamp, 1978), translated into English as *A Theory of Legal Argumentation* (Oxford: Clarendon Press, 1989).

3. Manuel Atienza, *Las razones del derecho: teorías de la argumentación jurídica* (Madrid: Centro de Estudios Constitucionales, 1989).

opposite reasons, will occupy the whole scene in Alexy's and Atienza's theories of juridical argumentation.

It is worth noting that Dworkin poses the question of interpretation starting from his quite precise and rigorous discussion of the paradox *hard cases* constitute for the most concrete juridical practice. Thus we are dealing with a strategy that takes its starting point in a perplexity arising at the point of the actual practice of a judge and, from there, rises to general considerations concerning the coherence of judicial practice.

It is along this route that the author of *A Matter of Principle* encounters the question of the relation between law and interpretation.

The privileged position accorded difficult cases in *A Matter of Principle* is not accidental. Hard cases already constituted a touchstone in Dworkin's *Taking Rights Seriously*[4] and in an essay I shall refer to below, "Is Law a System of Rules?" which is included in an anthology Dworkin edited, titled *The Philosophy of Law*.[5]

When is the judge confronted with a so-called hard case? When none of the legal dispositions drawn from existing laws seems to constitute the norm under which the affair in question might be placed. We could say, in Kantian language, that hard cases constitute a test for reflective judgment. Why then struggle with the tenacity and subtlety deployed by Dworkin against the thesis "no answer"? In order to checkmate the positivist theory of law, which is Dworkin's constant target. According to this latter, reduced to its bare skeleton, laws are said to be proclaimed by someone, in a position of command; they are therefore identified by their pedigree, the intention of the legislator constituting a corollary to this first axiom. What is more, they are said to govern unequivocal dispositions (one can see the hermeneutical question peeping through here inasmuch as this is partly bound to the irreducible equivocity of texts). Third axiom: if no response to the question posed seems to be contained in the law in force, then the judgment of the case is left to the discretionary power of the judge.

It is the refutation of these three master theses that will make a

---

4. Ronald Dworkin, *Taking Rights Seriously* (Cambridge: Harvard University Press, 1977).

5. Ronald Dworkin, *The Philosophy of Law* (New York: Oxford University Press, 1977).

bed for a theory of interpretation. In the first place, the meaning of a law does not result from its pedigree. As one would say in the terms of a nonintentional theory of the literary text, the meaning of a law, if it has one, is to be sought in the text and its intertextual connections, and not in the will of a legislator, juridically symmetrical with the intention attributed to the author of a literary text. Next, as admitted by positivist theorists such as H. L. A. Hart, the most explicit laws have an "open structure," in the sense of a text open to unforeseen constructive interpretations. But it is the refutation of the third thesis, that of the stand-in role granted to the discretionary power of the judge, that will directly open the way to a theory of interpretation. If the judge's "discretion" is the only reply to the silence of the law, then the alternative is fatal for every juridical characterization of a decision. Either it is arbitrary, in the sense of being outside the law, or it enters the law thanks only to the legislative claim with which it cloaks itself. Only the capacity to draw on a precedent preserves the juridical characterization of a decision stemming from any discretionary power.

Whence the problem as Dworkin sees it: how to justify the idea that there is always a valid response, without falling into the arbitrary or into the judge's claim to make himself a legislator?

It is at this critical instant that the juridical theory runs into the model of the literary text and the submodel of the narrative text, which will become, under Dworkin's pen, the paradigm of the literary text.

Let us pause a moment on the plane of the general theory of the literary text. The disjunction used in literary criticism between the meaning immanent to a text and the author's intention finds a parallel in juridical theory in the disjunction made between the meaning of a law and the instance of a decision that juridical positivism identifies as the source of a law. The literary enterprise takes on a canonical character for juridical theory as soon as interpretation finds a handhold in the permissions of the text, those it offers to the chain of its readers. What has been called the fuzziness or vagueness of a literary text becomes no longer a figure of weakness, but of strength, for what we can call symmetrically the "judicial enterprise."

It is now that the narrative model takes on a particular relief, to the extent that interpretation calls in a visible manner, in the reconstruction of the meaning of a text, on those relations of fittingness, of rightness, of adjustment between the proposed interpretation of a difficult passage and the overall interpretation of the work. One will recognize in this "fit" the well-known hermeneutical principle of the mutual interpretation of parts and whole. We shall see in a moment under what point of view the juridical enterprise allows itself to be better considered as a work that forms a whole.

But let us say that the evaluation of a relation of fittingness, of rightness, of adjustment escapes the alternative between demonstrability and arbitrariness. We are on a plane where controversy is certainly possible, but where a critic can claim that one interpretation is better than another, is more probable, more plausible, more acceptable (where all these terms need to be further clarified). What now appears is that the thesis "no answer" went hand in hand with the thesis of demonstrability; that is, says Dworkin, the thesis of a judgment supported by arguments whose truth will impose itself on whoever understands the language in which the juridical proposition is stated. It is perhaps at this point that Dworkin, blinded by the rival thesis of demonstrability, overlooks the moment where interpretation would call on a theory of argumentation that itself escapes the alternative of the demonstrable and the arbitrary. We can attribute this gap in reasoning to the perhaps excessive preoccupation attached to the refutation of the "no answer" thesis which ends up by instituting too rigid a connection between the solution of difficult cases and the thesis of the demonstrability of juridical propositions.

But let us push ahead the exploitation of the literary model in its more precisely narrative form. In what context must we place ourselves in order to see the search for an interpretive "fit" verified by what Dworkin calls the "facts of narrative coherence"? We have to leave behind the isolated case of some determinative judgment and place ourselves in the perspective of a history of the judicial enterprise, hence to take into account the temporal dimension of this enterprise. Here is where Dworkin has recourse to the fable of a chain of narrators, each one adding his chapter to the redaction of a story, where no one narrator determines the global meaning, which however each one must presume, if he adopts as a rule the search for maximal coherence. This anticipation of narrative coherence conjoined with the understanding of the preceding chapters of a story that each narrator finds already underway gives the search for a "fit" a double surety: that of precedents, on the one hand, and that of the presumed aim of the juridical whole in the course of elaboration, on the other. In other words, on one side, the already judged, on the other, the anticipated profile of the juridical enterprise considered in terms of its historicity. It is in this way that the model of the text—and more particularly of the narrative text—provides an acceptable alternative to the response "no answer" given to hard cases and, at the same time, to the positivist conception of law.

Unfortunately, Dworkin did not seize the occasion to coordinate his general notion of a "fit," and more precisely the narrativist notion of this fit, with a theory of argumentation that could have been taken up in terms of the very same criterion of coherence, whether this was or was not reducible to narrative coherence. The proposed synonyms—integrity, identity—do not add any particular precision to the overly indeterminate notion of coherence. At most, he appeals to concepts like those we find in Stephen Toulmin, such as weight, relevance, warrant, rebuttal, and so on,[6] all of which stem from an as yet inchoate theory of argumentation, as Alexy and Atienza will say.

So we can ask why Dworkin did not look on the side of a more refined theory of argumentation. It is certainly not due to a lack of subtlety, for he is a redoubtable debater, but instead for deeper reasons that we will understand better if we set the section "Law and Interpretation" in *A Matter of Principle* next to the essay "Is Law a System of Rules?" drawn from *The Philosophy of Law*. This essay reveals that Dworkin is much less interested in the formality of arguments than in their substance and, let us say straightaway, in their moral and political substance. The concept of law proposed in this remarkable article rests on a hierarchy of the various normative components of the law. It is again the quarrel with Hart's positivism that leads the way. What is denounced here is the complicity between the juridical rigidity attached to the idea of a univocal rule and the decisionism that ends up increasing a judge's discretionary power. Univocity, it is strongly emphasized, is a characteristic of *rules*. It does not fit *principles*, which, in the final analysis, are of an ethico-juridical nature. The established law, as a system of rules, does not exhaust the law as a political enterprise.

In what way does this distinction between principles and rules

---

6. Stephen Edelston Toulmin, *The Uses of Argument* (Cambridge: Cambridge University Press, 1969).

contribute to a hermeneutic theory of judicial judgment? It does so in that it is principles rather than rules that work together more readily toward the solution of hard cases. And these principles, unlike rules, are identifiable not by their pedigrees (who proclaimed them? Custom? The ruling power? An elusive legislature? Precedents?), but by their normative force. Next, unlike second-degree rules, such as Hart's "rules of recognition," their ethico-political status excludes univocality. In each case, they have to be interpreted. And each interpretation can be said to "count in favor of" this or that solution, "weigh" more or less, incline without necessitating, to speak like Leibniz. We have to speak of their weight, which has to be evaluated in each case. Above all, we have to test the "sense of appropriateness" that has developed in the history of the profession and of the educated public. With this, it is no longer possible to proceed to a complete enumeration of exceptions, any more than it is possible to make a complete survey of the principles in force. The vocabulary of many verdicts in common law—terms such as unreasonable, negligent, unjust, significant—marks the place for interpretation up to the pronouncement of the verdict.

One can understand that this supple, noncodifiable conception of interpretation would rebel against the formalism of a theory of juridical argumentation. Dworkin is much more interested in the ethico-political horizon against which the principles irreducible to rules stand out. He is willing to assume all the inconveniences: the interminable character of controversy, which is compensated for only by the strong consensus of a democratic society (here we rediscover the later Rawls and his "overlapping consensus"); the fragility of judgments handed over to the acceptance of different concerned audiences (the parties in the case, the judicial profession, legal theorists). Dworkin here rediscovers, without perhaps being aware of it, the difficulties raised in literary theory by the text-reception school.

But I do not want to leave Dworkin without having underscored the merits of his conception. He owes to the model of the text a conception of the law freed from what he calls its pedigree. From a model of narration, despite a certain naiveté in the face of the contemporary development of theories bearing on narrativity, he takes up "legal practice" in terms of its historical unfolding, "legal history" being set up as the interpretive framework. Finally, from the distinction between principles and rules, he draws a general conception of

law inseparable from "a substantive political theory." It is this ultimate and fundamental interest that finally distances him from a formal theory of juridical argumentation.

FROM ARGUMENTATION TO INTERPRETATION?

The strategy used by such specialists in the study of juridical argument as Alexy and Atienza is quite different. It is a matter, essentially, of treating this kind of argument as a special case of practical
normative discussion in general, hence of inscribing the small circle
of juridical argumentation within the larger circle of practical argumentation in general. Therefore it is by starting from the latter that
one undertakes the task of *Begründung,* that is, of justification or
foundation.[7]

So it is the turning point between two levels that matters, inasmuch as it is within the constraints and procedures particular to juridical argumentation that we may venture to find an occasion for
articulating interpretation on the basis of justification, even if our
authors only do this episodically (and, in this regard, Atienza provides more of a basis than does Alexy for such an attempt at reconciliation, as his consideration of those cases he calls "tragic" suggests).[8]

Let us begin therefore by spending some time on the plane of
normative practical discourse. All three terms deserve some explication. By "practical," one means the whole domain of human interactions. This latter is more precisely considered from the point of view
of the norms that govern it and that, as norms, make a claim to correctness (*Richtigkeit, rectitude, correción*). They do so through the exchange of arguments whose logic does not come down to mere
formal logic, yet without giving in to the arbitrariness of a decisionism nor to the alleged intuition of intuitionist moral theories, which
immediately casts a suspicious light on the concept of discretionary

7. The English-language translator chose the term "justification," the Spanish speaks
of "*fundamentación.*"

8. Let me say something about the vocabulary here. In German, especially in that of
Habermas and his school, *Diskurs* signifies both discourse in general, that is, the linking
together of sentences, and discourse in the sense of discussion, hence the linking together
of arguments. In the English translation we find "discourse," in Spanish "*discurso.*" In
French, the term *discours* readily takes on the sense of discussion based on arguments. This
is why we can speak of an ethics of discourse or of discussion.

power. The concept of "discourse" imposes a certain formalism, which is precisely that of argumentation, at the point where the terms "discourse" and "argumentation" tend to overlap.

The question, therefore, is how the claim to correctness gets defined. It is from Habermas and the Erlangen School that one borrows the answer: correctness is the claim raised for intelligibility, as soon as it admits the criterion of universalizable communicability. A good argument is one that ideally will be understood, taken not only as plausible, but as acceptable by all the parties concerned. We recognize here the Habermasian thesis of a potential agreement at the level of an unlimited and unconstrained community. It is against this horizon of universal consensus that we are to place the formal rules of every discussion claiming correctness. These rules, which we shall see are relatively few in number, constitute what is essential to a universal pragmatics of discourse, where the normative accent needs to be strongly emphasized, over against any reduction to the strategic argumentation that governs negotiation, which is bound by constraints of many different types and aims at success, not at correctness.

To the objection that comes immediately to mind, that such a consensus is beyond reach, unrealizable, the response is precisely that the counterfactual character of the idea of correctness legitimates its transcendental status, which assimilates it to an endless task. To the objection that this foundation by itself is insufficient, the response is that it is precisely the task of the theory of juridical argumentation to complete the set of general rules of normative discourse in a particular field, that of the law. To the objection, finally, that in virtue of its ideal character, the theory of argumentation may serve as an alibi for systematic distortions, the response is that the ideal of a potential agreement contains within itself the conditions for a rational critique of more or less empirical agreements, due more or less to extortion, stemming from coalitions of interests, and in general representative of any factual equilibrium between conflicting powers.

If we ask for a more precise statement of the modes of this pragmatics, which now can be formulated, we learn that the possible universalization of an argument is where its correctness lies. We shall see below what this means on the juridical plane. Does this mean we are limited here to repeating what Kant says? No, reply the Haber-

masians, the principle of universalizability is here applied in an immediately dialogical situation, whereas for Kant it remains confined
to an inner monologue (something, let me note in passing, that is
highly contestable and certainly wrong with respect to the Kantian
philosophy of right).

As was said above, the rules of this pragmatics are few in number.
But they suffice for an ethics of discussion. Some govern the entry
into discourse, let us say, of beginning to speak out: everyone has an
equal right to intervene, no one is prevented from speaking. Other
rules apply to a discussion as it unfolds: each participant must accept
the demand made upon him to give reasons and, if possible, the best
argument, or to justify his refusal to do so. This rule constitutes the
general rule of justification. Other rules govern what is at issue in the
discussion: everyone must accept the consequences of a decision if
everyone's well-argued-for needs have been satisfied. Note: this last
rule is already an indication of the turning point from the formal to
the substantial (or material) in virtue of the recourse made to the notions of a need or an interest.[9] It is here that something like an interpretation gets inserted into the discussion once needs or interests
depend on understanding or evaluation, and once (if they are to be
understood or accepted) they have passed the initial test of a shared
evaluation of some community or communities of varying size.[10]
Insofar as we are here straightaway on the plane of communicability,
it is in terms of *shared understandings* that interests and needs enter
into any rule-governed discussion. Formal normativity cannot do
without the presumed normativity through which some particular
position announces itself as debatable, that is, in a sense properly
speaking as plausible. This aspect of debatability underlies ideas like
Offenheit (openness, *apertura*). Finally, a decision taken within some
limited discursive framework is submitted to conditions of acceptability on the plane of what Perelman called a universal audience.[11]

9. We find here a situation comparable to that found in John Rawls's *Theory of Justice*
once it is a question of "fundamental social goods" to be distributed.

10. We find here the equivalent of the Kantian notion of a maxim, which corresponds
to the fact that empirical desires must have taken on a certain generality, let us say that of
an action plan, even of a life plan, if they are to be able to lend themselves to the criteria of
universalization.

11. Chaim Perelman, *Le raisonnable et le déraisonnable en droit* (Brussels: Editions de
l'Université de Bruxelles, 1984); *Traité de l'argumentation. La nouvelle rhétorique* (1988);
Ethique et droit (1990).

In fact, a whole series of audiences are concerned here, having to do with the reception by other discursive instances, themselves affected in concretely different ways by the claim to correctness (or correction).

At the end of this quick sketch of the constitutive rules of rational practical discourse in general, we can certainly see that, owing to its counterfactual character, the notion of an ideal discourse situation offers a horizon of correctness for all discourse where the participants seek to convince each other through argument. The ideal is not just anticipated, it is already at work. But we must also emphasize that the formal can be inserted into the course of a discussion only if it is articulated on the basis of already public expressions of interests, hence of needs marked by prevailing interpretations concerning their legitimacy, and as contributing to what above we called their debatable character. It is here that Alexy himself introduces (but without dwelling upon it) the notion of interpretation, when he refers to the rules governing "the interpretation of one's own and others' needs as being generalizable or not."[12] Admitting this does not constitute a fatal concession to the formalism of pure theory inasmuch as one insists on the fact that it is from within a discourse that the protagonists raise a claim concerning the correctness of their discourse. So here is where we come up against the question of what is discursively possible in a given historical situation. Without this, we could not even speak of a capacity to render things problematic, presupposed—and required—by each of the protagonists in a discussion.

The time has come to characterize juridical discourse as a particular species of the genus of practical discourse in general.

We must first recall the diversity of places where juridical discourse occurs, before speaking of the specific limitations on such discourse. The *judicial* instance, which I shall take as the paradigmatic case, with its courts, tribunals, and judges, is just one of the places where juridical discourse takes place. Beyond it, there is the legislative instance, which produces laws, and alongside it, that of legal theorists, who express themselves through what German jurists call juridical dogmatics and what in English falls under the heading of jurisprudence and the philosophy of law. We should add to this,

---

12. Alexy, *A Theory of Legal Argumentation*, 133.

following Perelman, public opinion and, at the limit, the universal audience to which theories of jurisprudence, laws coming from legislative bodies, and finally the decisions issued by the judiciary are submitted. Of all these cases, it is court decisions that are subject to the strictest constraints, constraints that are likely to force a gap between practical discourse in general and judicial discourse. It is these constraints I want to take up now.

In the first place, the discussion takes place in a particular institutional setting (tribunals and courts). In this setting, not every question is open to debate, only those that fall within the codified framework of a trial or lawsuit. In the trial itself, the roles are not equally distributed (the accused is not voluntarily present; he is summoned). Furthermore, the deliberation is subject to procedural rules that are themselves codified. Let us also add that the deliberation takes place over a limited timespan, unlike in jurisprudence or, up to a certain point, the deliberations of a legislative body. Finally, the discussion in the judicial instance does not end with an agreement and does not even aim at one, at least as a first approximation. Judgment means a decision and therefore a separation of the parties, instituting, has I have said elsewhere, a just distance between them. Hence we must not lose sight of the legal obligation that weighs on the judge, to render a judgment.

Within these constraining conditions, what happens to normative discourse in general? Alexy and those who uphold what it is convenient to call the standard theory emphasize the connection by filiation starting from the claim to correctness common to all normative discourse, before beginning to weigh the specific characters of juridical discourse. Their thesis is that the claim to correctness of a juridical argument in no way differs from that of normative discourse in general. The general norm is implicit. Ideally the person who loses, the one condemned, is included in the recognition of this claim assumed to be shared by all the parties involved. This implicit presupposition is expressed in some juridical systems by the obligation to motivate the decision. But even if the decision is not publicly motivated, it is at least justified by the arguments employed. This is why a judge cannot both rule on a case and at the same time declare that his sentence is unjust. This performative contradiction is as blatant as the one where someone says that the cat is on the mat, without actually believing it.[13] This thesis itself depends on an argument *a contrario:* if juridical argumentation did not have normative discourse in general aiming at correctness as its horizon, no meaning could be given to the idea of arguing rationally. Therefore if new constraints have to be added to the theory of normative discussion, they must fit with the formal rules without weakening them.

This having been said, what place is there for interpretation? Recourse from argumentation to interpretation seems to me to impose itself starting on the plane Alexy characterizes as "internal justification," in order to oppose it to "external justification." Internal justification has to do with the logical coherence between premises and conclusion. Thus it characterizes argumentation as a kind of inference.

In my opinion, the juridical syllogism cannot simply be reduced to the direct way of subsumption of a case under a rule; rather, it must further satisfy a criterion of recognition of the appropriate character of the application of this norm to this case. We find here something like the rule of "fit" referred to by Dworkin. The application of a rule is in fact a very complex operation where the interpretation of the facts and the interpretation of the norm mutually condition each other, before ending in the qualification by which it is said that some allegedly criminal behavior falls under such and such a norm which is said to have been violated. If we begin with the interpretation of the facts, we cannot overemphasize the multitude of ways a set of interconnected facts can be considered and, let us say, recounted. Here we ought to enlarge the investigation to include the whole practical field Wilhelm Schapp covers in his *In Geschichten verstrickt.*[14] We never finish untangling the lines of the personal story of an accused with certainty, and even reading it in such a way is already oriented by the presumption that such an interconnectedness places the case under some rule. To say that *a* is a case of *B* is already to decide that the juridical syllogism holds for it. This syllo-

---

13. One immediate application comes to mind here. On the penal plane, no educational project, no concern for the resocialization of the condemned will be justified, and perhaps none can be efficacious, if the condemned person is not treated as a rational being, capable at a minimum of understanding the arguments opposed to his criminal behavior.

14. Wilhlem Schapp, *In Geschichten verstrickt* (Wiesbaden: B. Heymann, 1976; Vittorio Kostermann, 1983). *Empêtré dans des histoires,* trans. Jean Greisch (Paris: Cerf, 1992).

gism is juridical and not merely practical because the subsumption in question is itself a problem. Does it suffice to say, as do the upholders of argument theory, that it is necessary to add some supplementary rules? Alexy writes here: "Whenever it is open to doubt whether *a* is a T or an M, a rule must be put forward which settles this question."[15] His argument is based on the rule of universalization. If there were not some means of assuring ourselves that *a*, like *b*, like *c*, is a case of *D* we would violate the rule of universalization. Therefore we must proceed by degrees to decompose things until we find a use of the expressions of the law whose application to a given case leaves no place for dispute.

But can this wholly formal condition always be met? Can subsumption, even in terms of decomposed degrees, take place without a conjoint interpretation of the norm and the facts through their being mutually adjusted to one another? I will say, for my part, that interpretation has become the *organon* of inference. To put it in Kantian terms: interpretation is the path followed by the productive imagination in the operation of the reflective judgment. The question this poses is as follows: under what rule should a particular case be placed? Universalization, then, only provides a check on the process of mutual adjustment between the interpreted norm and the interpreted fact. In this sense, interpretation is not external to argumentation. It constitutes its *organon*. Even the idea of similar cases rests on the interpretation of an analogy. This is why we must always interpret at the same time the norm as covering a case and the case as covered, if the juridical syllogism is to work, which, then, does not differ in any way from the practical syllogism.[16] I conclude that interpretation is incorporated into justification beginning on the level Alexy calls internal justification, where the logical coherence alone of the inference is at issue.

Whatever the case may be about the role of interpretation on the most formal plane of juridical inference, it is at the level of what Alexy calls external justification, that is, the justification of the

16. Authors such as Engisch and Larenz, cited by Alexy (ibid., 228, n. 44), emphasize the role of "discovery" in the operation of justification and speak in this regard of a juridical hermeneutics. Alexy sets this moment of discovery on the side of a psychological description of the trial, disjoining it from justification. But does juridical argumentation not have as its first characteristic that it does not separate discovery and justification?

premises, that the interweaving of argumentation and interpretation seems to me most indisputable.

Let us first recall that the most fundamental limitation juridical argumentation meets has to do with the fact that the judge is not a legislator, that he applies the law, that is, he incorporates into his arguments the law in effect. Here is where we rediscover the vague character of juridical language, the possible conflicts among norms, the provisory silence of the law about Dworkin's "hard cases," the opportunity and often the necessity to choose between the spirit and the letter of the law. It is in applying it that we not only recognize the norm as constraining, but test its variability, and that the interplay between the double interpretation of law and facts described above is most clear.[17]

In the second rank we have to place the hazards and the trial and error of properly empirical investigation. Here is an occasion to recall that the interpretation of what counts as a fact, and as a relevant fact within the radius of the investigation of the case in question, has to do to the same degree with the justification said to be internal and that said to be external. The "facts" in a case, not just their evaluation but their very description, are the object of multiple legal disputes where, once again, the interpretation of the norm and that of these facts overlap. Here again, it is legitimate to refer to Dworkin when he emphatically repeats that the "facts" in a case are not brute facts but charged with meaning, hence interpreted.

In the third place, still on the plane of justification of the premises, we can place recourse to and borrowings from juridical theory, what Alexy calls legal dogmatics. Here there is a parallel to the distinction introduced by Dworkin between rule and principle. We have noted with Dworkin how recourse to principles differs from recourse to rules. The rule constrains; principles "incline," they "weigh" more or less heavily in favor of a thesis.

It is at this stage that we can understand the recourse to what,

17. One can, of course, isolate what some authors call "special juridical arguments," such as analogy, argument *a contrario, a fortiori*, by absurdity, and so forth. But if these operate on the boundary of the formal and the substantial, there is nothing specific about them as regards the law. We also find them in other spheres of discourse. Even so, Alexy and other authors reformulate them in terms of the framework of logical inference. In this regard, what happens to analogy is particularly exemplary: "it relies on the principle of universalizability which is constitutive of both general practical and legal discourse" (ibid., 283).

since *System of Contemporary Roman Law* (1840) by F. C. Savigny, have been called "canons of interpretation." We can certainly give them a formal version by saying that they consist of interpreting norm *N* in terms of weight *W.* This interpretation can be reduced to a simple semantic argument, but it may also set in motion a "genetic" argument once the intention of the legislator is invoked in connection with the distinction between the spirit and the letter of the law. Here again Alexy intersects with Dworkin without recognizing it. Nothing is more subject to challenge than the invocation of the intention of the legislator. Did the legislator want us to interpret *N* in terms of *W*? Did he have in mind some goal beyond the norm *N*? It is in this way, by referring to one reason among others, that an argument invoking the intention of the legislator has to be "weighed." In any case, were it to be known, even such an intention itself is not univocal. In this respect, all the "genetic" arguments, or arguments about "pedigree," as Dworkin says, have to be placed under the same rubric as the historical or comparative arguments. In the end, recourse to theory and to so-called systematic arguments does not get us away from hermeneutics, but rather in a strange way leads back toward it owing to its multiple aspects of plurivocity.

In the final analysis, a particular outcome must be assigned to the preceding argument.[18] In one sense, it does not have to do with external justification inasmuch as a precedent, once recognized as a similar case, brings into play no other criterion than its capacity for universalization (treat similar cases similarly). However, it is the recognition of similitude that poses a problem. To say that some solution is a precedent is already to make some selection in the *thesaurus* of legal rulings. And in terms of what aspect are two cases similar? We are back to the respective "weighing" of resemblances and differences. And if agreement is reached concerning these, the question remains: which resemblances and which differences are relevant to the case under consideration? One can, of course, adopt as a rule expecting more from the argumentation of the one who challenges an already established precedent and pleads for an exception. In this regard, Perelman referred to a kind of principle of inertia that applies to the appeal to precedent. In light of the inertia of established judgments, there must be good reasons for deviating

18. Cf. ibid., 274–79.

from the acquired way of interpreting things. A precedent assures the stability, security, and confidence of a decision. Here, though, the formalists observe that this overly sociological justification of recourse to precedent does not solve the problem of the argumentative structure of the appeal to precedent. They are correct. But it is precisely this argumentative structure that sets the interpretation in motion. The precedent appeals back to similarity, which is neither given nor invented, but constructed. In Dworkin's vocabulary, it is a case of constructive interpretation. Whether one argues for or against assumes that one tries out in imagination the hypothesis of resemblance or difference.

Finally, we must no doubt make a place, as Atienza recommends, for insoluble cases given the present state of the law. Dworkin undoubtedly goes too far in affirming that there is always a right answer to the question posed by hard cases, in order to block the invasive recourse to discretionary power in a positivist conception of law. The tragic cases Atienza willingly discusses in effect call on a sense of justice or equity that is difficult to formalize, or, one might say, on a sense of justness more than justice.

At the conclusion of this discussion perhaps my reader will grant that the interweaving of argumentation and interpretation on the judicial plane is indeed symmetrical to that between explanation and understanding on the plane of the sciences of discourse and of the text. Over against an approach to this well-known polarity in terms of a pure dichotomy, I have elsewhere concluded my plea for their dialectical treatment with an aphoristic formula: to explain more in order to understand better. In concluding my discussion of the debate over interpretation and argumentation, I want to propose a similar formula that will restore a complex unity to the epistemology of the judicial debate. The point where interpretation and argumentation overlap is the one where Dworkin's regressive and ascending way and Alexy and Atienza's progressive and descending way intersect. The former finds its starting point in the difficult question posed by hard cases and from there rises toward the ethico-political horizon of the "judicial enterprise" considered in terms of its historical unfolding. The latter proceeds from a general theory of argumentation valid for every form of normative practical discussion and encounters juridical argument as a subordinate province. The first way reaches the common crossroads at the moment when the theory of interpretation encounters the question posed by the narrative model of criteria of coherence applying to judgment in juridical matters. The second reaches it when, in order to account for the specificity of juridical argumentation, procedures of interpretation again find their relevance as the *organon* of the juridical syllogism thanks to which a case is placed under a rule. I even went so far as to risk a suggestion of another analogy besides the dialectic between explanation and understanding, namely, that of the reflective judgment in the sense of Kant's *Critique of Judgment*, interpretation becoming the way the productive imagination follows once the problem is no longer to apply a known rule to a presumably correctly described case, as with determinative judgment, but to "find" a rule *under* which it is appropriate to place a fact that itself must be interpreted. Then it becomes a question of showing that we do not really change problematics when we pass from the analogy between the pair "to interpret/to argue" and the pair "to understand/to explain" to the analogy with reflective judgment. This will be the object of another discussion whose echo can be found in another essay in this collection.[19]

19. Cf. the previous chapter, "Aesthetic Judgment and Political Judgment According to Hannah Arendt." There I suggest that the Kantian theory of reflective judgment illustrated in the third Critique by the analysis of the judgment of taste and that of the teleological judgment can receive other applications than those proposed by Kant, by following the way opened by Arendt in her unfinished work on judging. The epistemology of judicial debate may constitute another of these extensions beyond Kant's own framework, alongside, for example, historical judgment and medical judgment.

The Act of Judging

It is at the endpoint of the arguments that make up a trial that I want to place myself in order to take up the subject proposed here. Indeed, it is at the end of deliberation that the act of judgment takes place. It is a kind of phenomenology of this act that I want to propose for discussion.

I shall distinguish a short-term end, in virtue of which judging signifies deciding, with an eye to ending uncertainty; to this I shall oppose a long-term end, undoubtedly more concealed—namely, the contribution of a judgment to public peace. It is the path from this short-term end to the long-term end that I want to discuss.

Let us begin by saying that judging is deciding. This initial finality leaves the act of judging, in the judicial sense of the word (that is, to give a ruling as a judge) within the range of nontechnical, nonjudicial meanings of the act of judging, whose components and criteria I want briefly to recall.

In the usual sense of the word, the verb *to judge* covers a range of major senses that I propose to arrange in what I shall call an order of increasing density. First, in a weak sense, to judge is to opine. However, an opinion is expressed about something. In a slightly stronger sense, to judge is to value, to assess. In this way, a hierarchical element is introduced, expressing a preference, an evaluation, an approbation. A third degree of force expresses the encounter between the subjective and the objective sides of judgment. Objective side: someone takes a proposition as true, good, just, legal; subjective side: he subscribes to it. Finally, at a deeper level than the one assumed by Descartes in his Fourth Meditation, judgment proceeds from the conjunction between understanding and will. The understanding that considers the true and false—the will that decides. In this way we have reached the strong sense of the word "judge": not just to opine, value, take as true, but in the final analysis, to take a stand. It is from this ordinary sense of the word that we can depart to rejoin the properly judicial sense of the act of judging.

With the judicial sense, judgment in effect intervenes in social practice, at the level of that exchange of discourse Jürgen Habermas links to communicative activity, thanks to the central phenomenon of this social practice constituted by the trial in a law court. It is within the framework of the trial that the act of judging recapitulates all the ordinary senses: opine, assess, take as true or false, and finally, take a stand.

The question then arises under what conditions the act of judging in its judicial form can be said to be authorized or competent. In my essay "Le juste entre le légal et le bon,"[1] I considered four such conditions:

1. the existence of written laws;

2. the presence of an institutional framework: courts, appeal courts, and so on;

3. the intervention of qualified, competent, independent persons, who we say are "charged with judging";

4. finally, a course of action constituted by the trial process, referred to above, where the pronouncement of judgment constitutes the endpoint.

Of course, beyond this point—well named in French: *arrêt*—it is always possible to deliberate, in the sense that every judgment calls for a "but" beyond itself. However, it is a characteristic of judgment on the judicial plane to interrupt the back-and-forth play of arguments by giving them an endpoint, even if this latter is provisory, at least so long as the ways of appeal remain open. But there will ultimately be a place or moment where a final ruling is sanctioned by public force.

Before showing why we cannot limit ourselves to this definition of the act of judging, entirely delimited by the conditions of the trial process, it is important to emphasize the social necessity attached to that finality we have called short-term, consisting in the interruption of uncertainty. Within the strict limits of the trial process, the act of judging appears as the terminal phase of a drama with several actors: the parties or their representatives, the public attorney, the judge, the jury, and so on. What is more, this terminal act appears as the closure of an unpredictable process. In this regard, there is something here like a game of chess. The rules of the game are known, but in each instance one does not know how the game will reach its end. The trial is to the law what a game of chess is to the rules of chess. In both cases, one has to get to the end to know the result. This is how a ruling puts an end to a virtually endless deliberation. And despite the limitations I shall speak of in a moment, the act of judging, by suspending the hazards of the trial, expresses the force of law; what is more, it states the law in terms of a singular situation.

It is through the twofold relation it has with the law that this act of judging expresses the force of law. On the one side, in effect, it seems simple to apply the law to a case. We have what Kant calls a determinative judgment. But there is also the question of an interpretation of the law, insofar as no case is simply the exemplification of a rule. To use Kantian language again, we can say that act of judging stems from a reflective judgment, itself consisting in seeking a rule for a new case. In this second sense, the ruling is not limited to ending a trial. It opens the way to a whole course of jurisprudence insofar as it creates a precedent. The suspending aspect of the act of judging at the end of a deliberative course therefore does not exhaust the meaning of this act.

Before expanding on my thesis, I want also to say that, considered in terms of the strict limits of the trial process, the exercise of the act of judging easily finds a place in the general functioning of society, considered by Rawls as a vast system for distributing shares. Indeed, it is under the aegis of the idea of distributive justice that the act of judging can be represented. In effect, a given society develops a scheme for passing out shares, which are not all measured in monetary terms assignable to the commercial order. A given society distributes goods of all kinds, those that can be exchanged and those that cannot. Taken in a broad sense, the act of judging consists in separating spheres of activity, in delimiting the claims of the one from those of the other, and finally in correcting unjust distributions, when the activity of one party encroaches on the field of exercise of other parties. In this respect, the act of judging certainly consists in separating. The German term *Urteil* expresses this well (*Teil* means part). It is indeed a matter of deciding the part of one and that of another. The act of judging is therefore one of *dé-partage,* one that *sé-pare,* that separates. In saying this, I am saying nothing out of the ordinary inasmuch as the ancient Roman definition *suum cuique tribuere*—to attribute to each his own—was implicitly oriented toward the analysis proposed here. What is more, the whole of Kant's philosophy of right rests on this distinction between "mine" and "yours," on the act that draws a line between the one and the other.

These latter considerations have to do with the act of deciding, in the sense of separating, of opening the way to the decisive expansion announced at the beginning of this lecture. Why, in fact, can we not stop with what I have called the short-term finality of the act of judging, that is, with putting an end to uncertainty? Because the trial process itself is only the codified form of a broader phenomenon, namely, that of conflict. It is a question therefore of replacing the trial process, with its precise procedures, against the background of the broader social phenomenon inherent in the functioning of civil society and situated at the origin of public discussion.

This is where we have to go. Behind the trial process lies conflict, differences of opinion, quarrels, litigation—and behind conflict lies violence. The place of justice is marked out in a provisionary manner in this way, as being part of the set of alternatives that a society opposes to violence and that at the same time defines a State of right. In *Lectures I* I paid homage to Eric Weil, who introduced his great work, *Logique de la philosophie,* with a long meditation on the relation between discourse and violence. In a way, all the operations I have referred to, from deliberation to rendering a decision to passing judgment, manifest the choice of discourse over violence.

We get a sense of the importance of this choice against violence and for discourse only if we remind ourselves of the scope of the phenomenon of violence. It would be wrong to reduce violence to aggression, even when broadened beyond physical aggression: blows, wounds, death, a restriction on freedom, detention, and so on. We need also to take into account the most tenacious form of violence, namely, vengeance, or, in other words, an individual's claim to procure justice by himself. At bottom, justice is opposed not just to violence per se, or even to concealed violence or all the subtle forms just alluded to, but to that simulation of justice constituted by vengeance, the act of procuring justice by oneself. In this sense, the fundamental act by means of which we can speak of justice is founded on a society; it is the act by which society raises individuals to the level of right and law and the power to obtain justice for themselves—the act by which public power confiscates for itself the power to pronounce and to apply the law. What is more, it is in virtue of this confiscation that the most civilized operations of justice, in particular in the penal sphere, still bear the visible imprint of this original violence that is vengeance. In many respects, punishment, especially if it preserves some aspect of the old idea of expiation, remains an attenuated, filtered, civilized form of vengeance. This persistence of violence as vengeance means that we only accede to the sense of justice through the detour of the protest against injustice. The cry "Unfair!" often expresses an insightful intuition concerning the true nature of society, and the place violence still holds in it, as well as regards all rational or reasonable discourse about justice.

Having come to this point, we arrive at the question of the ultimate finality of the act of judging. Returning to our analysis of the act of judging starting from the far-reaching operation that consisted in the State taking from individuals the direct exercise of justice, and in the first place of vengeance as the means of justice, it turns out that the horizon of the act of judging is finally something more than security—it is *social peace*. How does this ultimate finality throw any light on our initial definition of the act of judging in terms of its short-term finality, that is, its putting an end to uncertainty through the act of rendering a decision? To decide, we said, is to separate, to draw a line between "yours" and "mine." The finality of social peace makes apparent something more profound that has to do with mutual recognition. Let us not say reconciliation; even less ought we to speak of love and pardon, which are not juridical categories. Let us speak instead of recognition. But in what sense? I think that the act of judging reaches its goal when someone who has, as we say, won his case still feels able to say: my adversary, the one who lost, remains like me a subject of right, his cause should have been heard, he made plausible arguments and these were heard. However, such recognition will not be complete unless the same thing can also be said by the loser, the one who did wrong, who has been condemned. He should be able to declare that the sentence that condemns him was not an act of violence but rather one of recognition.

To what vision of society does this reflection lead us? Somewhere beyond, I think, the conception of society as distributing shares, which do always need to be apportioned in order to determine which ones belong to this or that person. This would be the vision of society as a model of social cooperation. After all, this expression appears in the opening lines of John Rawls's *Theory of Justice,* a work in which nevertheless it is the analysis of society as a system of distribution that carries the day. The question is worth asking: what is it that makes society something more than a system of distribution? Or better: what is it that makes distribution a means of cooperation? Here is where a more substantial element than pure procedural justice has to be taken into account, namely, something like a common good, consisting in shared values. We are then dealing with a communitarian dimension underlying the purely procedural dimension of the societal structure. Perhaps we may even find in the metaphor of sharing the two aspects I am here trying to coordinate in terms of each other. In sharing there are shares, that is, those things that separate us. My share is not yours. But sharing is also what makes us share, that is, in the strong sense of the term, share in. . . .

I conclude then that the act of judging has as its horizon a fragile equilibrium of these two elements of sharing: that which separates my share or part from yours and that which, on the other hand, means that each of us shares in, takes part in society.

It is the just distance between partners who confront one another, too closely in cases of conflict and too distantly in those of ignorance, hate, and scorn, that sums up rather well, I believe, the two aspects of the act of judging. On the one hand, to decide, to put an end to uncertainty, to separate the parties; on the other, to make each party recognize the share the other has in the same society, thanks to which the winner and the loser of any trial can be said to have their fair share in that model of cooperation that is society.

Sanction, Rehabilitation, Pardon

The organizers of the colloquy "Justice or Vengeance?"[1] have given me the task of introducing the section placed under the aegis of the three words "sanction, rehabilitation, pardon." The contribution of a philosopher seems to me to be, here as in analogous situations, that of offering an analysis, one intended to offer some conceptual clarification, to help us recognize what is at stake, and finally to distinguish its ends. As a first approximation, then, it is a trajectory that is proposed for our examination, a trajectory that begins with sanction (that is, someone is condemned), that continues, in certain circumstances and within certain precise limits which we have yet to spell out, in a project of restoration (that is, someone is reestablished in his rights, with a civic or legal status that has been lost), and finally, in still more specific circumstances, that ends in making someone the beneficiary of a pardon that is not owed to him. His punishment is ended, he is reestablished in terms of both public esteem and self-esteem.

All this is a first approximation.

One doubt may immediately come to mind: is it a question of a continuous trajectory? Are the instances authorized for sanction, rehabilitation, and pardon all the same? To this can be added a connected doubt: is it a question of one and the same, continually passive subject, concerning whom we say that he *is* sanctioned, that he *is* rehabilitated, that he *is* pardoned? In order to respond to these doubts we have to move back to the beginning. What presents itself as the first term of the discontinuous and unpredictable triad of sanction, rehabilitation,

---

1. *Justice ou vengeance,* a discussion presented April 30, 1994, under the auspices of the magazine *La Croix, l'Evénement* (Paris: Editions du Centurion, 1994), 93–107.

and pardon is in terms of the reality of the judicial experience the last theme of a better interconnected sequence, along which what is at stake in our interrogation gets decided and takes on substance—namely, the difference between vengeance and justice. At the moment of pronouncing the sentence, something essential has already been decided: the verdict. The subject who has formally been held to be innocent (until proven guilty) has been declared guilty, hence punishable, hence subject to the punishment about to be announced. Because our proposed trajectory gets under way too late, it has left behind it the break that preoccupies us here—that between justice and vengeance.

The reason is that this break takes place before the sentence in the trial process. And the sentence itself only makes sense as a penalty because it closes and ends the trial. Therefore it is in terms of the structure of the trial process, as it ought to unfold within a State of right, that we have to seek the principle of the break between vengeance and justice. Sometimes we say that to avenge oneself is to obtain justice for oneself. But no, the word "justice" should not figure in any definition of vengeance, making allowance for the archaic and sacred sense of justice which is through and through vindictive and vengeful, which we do have to make sense of in the final analysis. For the moment, we have to do only with elementary, emotional, savage vengeance, the kind that wants to inscribe the punishment in the wake of the crime. The question thus arises by what means, with what resources, in the name of what principle the trial process breaks with this kind of vengeance.

Before dividing this process into its structural elements, we can characterize it overall in the following terms. It consists in establishing a *just distance* between the hideous crime that unleashes private and public anger, and the punishment inflicted by the judicial institution. Whereas vengeance short-circuits the two forms of suffering, that undergone by the victim and that inflicted by the avenger, the trial process gets interposed between these two, instituting the just distance we have just spoken of.

I

So our question is to recapitulate the means by which the exercise of penal law establishes the gap between violence and the word of justice.[2] Four elements appear to make up the structural conditions of every judicial hearing.

(1) First of all is that a third party, not party to the hearing and qualified to open a space of discussion, is presupposed. Under this general heading of a third party we can set three distinct cases: first, the institution of a State distinct from civil society and, in this regard, the guardian of legitimate violence (where multiple historical variations are capable of expressing this relationship between state power and civil society depending on the nature of the consensus established among the groups making up this latter); second, our conception of the judicial institution as distinct from other powers of the State (here again the relation can vary according to the model of separation of powers or authorities); to which we must not fail to add as a third aspect making up this third party the particular mode of recruiting judicial personnel. Here the third party takes on the human figure of the judge. It is important to set this out from the beginning inasmuch as judges are human beings like us, but raised above us in order to decide conflicts, at the end of qualifying tests meant to help ensure the acceptability of the verdict, something we shall discuss in greater detail below.

(2) Our third party does not find himself set in the required nonpartisan position except when backed by a juridical system consisting essentially of written laws, their inscription and conservation representing a considerable cultural acquisition thanks to which state power and judicial power are conjointly established. It is up to the laws on the one hand to define crimes, and on the other to establish a proportion between crime and punishment. The first operation contributes to bringing about a distance from violence by making possible the use of the qualification "crime" as applied to infractions defined and named in the most unequivocal way possible. Furthermore, the establishment of a double scale of crimes and punishments, on the basis of a rule of proportionality, when added to the qualification of what counts as a crime, allows any incriminated act to be situated with the greatest possible precision, not just on the chart but also on the scale of crimes.

(3) Next comes the essential element that gives the whole structure its title, namely, the *hearing.* Its function is to carry the pending case from a state of uncertainty to one of certitude. To do this, it is impor-

2. For the following analysis I draw upon Denis Salas, *Du procès pénal* (Paris: Presses Universitaires de France, 1992), 214–42.

tant that the hearing bring into play a plurality of protagonists who together—judge, public prosecutor, attorneys for the parties involved—contribute to setting up what I am calling a just distance, this time between the defendant and the accuser. This consideration of a plurality of protagonists in the hearing adds an important correction to the simple idea of a judging third party. The gap set up by this basic unit of the hearing transforms the flesh-and-blood victim, as well as the presumed guilty party, into "parties in the trial process," into accuser and defendant. But we have not yet spoken of what is most essential. It is important that the hearing be oral and confrontational, and established as such by a known procedure imposed on every protagonist in the hearing. In this way the hearing presents itself as a war of words: argument against argument, the arms being the same and equal on both sides. Finally, we must not omit underlining that the passive subject of our first approximation—someone *is* judged—is promoted by the hearing into an *actor* in the trial process. Below, we shall consider the importance of this mutation, when we run through the proposed sequence from sentence to rehabilitation to pardon.

(4) One last word about the fourth structural component of the trial process: the *verdict*. With it, guilt is legally established. With it, the accused changes juridical status from presumed innocent to declared guilty (or not guilty). This mutation is a result of the performative virtue of the speech act that *states the law* in some determined circumstance. I want to insist, at the end of this first section, on this expression: to state the law. I will consider below the therapeutic virtue to be found along the path of rehabilitation; even before that, however, the speech act that states the law already has numerous effects. It brings an end to uncertainty; it assigns the parties in the trial places that determine the just distance between vengeance and justice; finally, and perhaps above all, it recognizes as actors those persons who are accused of the offense and who stand to suffer the penalty. In this very effect lies the most significant reply given by justice to vengeance. It sums up the suspending of vengeance.

II

It is now possible to return to the sequence we proposed to examine: sanction-rehabilitation-pardon.

Sanction

We have not yet spoken of what is essential concerning the *sanction* as qualifying the final act of the trial process as the sentencing. The punishment has certainly taken on its penal aspect, at the end of the ceremony in language whereby the rupture with vengeance is consummated and whereby violence is poured into language. Yes, the "punishment" has been set at a just distance from the "crime." But we have not said to whom the sanction is due, who are its addressees. It is the answer to this question that gives meaning to the sentence as a penal sanction.

If we review again the structural components of the trial process, we have to say that the sanction is due in the first place to the law; not certainly due to the law rather than to the victim, but owed to the victim because it is due to the law. Kant and Hegel join hands on this point with the idea that the sanction *restores* the law. For the one as for the other, the law expresses the body of moral conventions that assures the minimal consensus of the political body, a consensus summed up in the idea of order. With regard to this order, every infraction is an attack against the law, something that upsets order. We can give a religious version of this idea, where one ties the law to an immutable, divinely guaranteed order. However, a profane version has bit by bit been substituted for the idea of an offense against the gods and taken the form of a secularized idea of a disturbed social order, of a threatened public peace. In both versions of such transgression, the punishment has as its first function to mend a public disorder, in short, to reestablish order. Hegel gives this process the dialectical form of a negation of negation. To the disorder that negates order responds the negation of disorder that reestablishes order (*The Philosophy of Right*).

Having said this, we cannot avoid the question in what sense the sanction can be said to be owed to the victim. The answer seems self-evident. Is it not to a flesh-and-blood person more than to some abstract law that reparation is due? Of course. Nevertheless, it remains necessary to say how this reparation is distinguished once again from vengeance. Must we not here pass through a point of doubt, suggested by the disillusioned comment of the sage meditating on the doubtful validity of all forms of punishment? Do not these, in the cosmic sum of rights and wrongs, add more suffering to suffering? Is punishing not, essentially, and in one way or another, a way of making someone suffer? And what are we to say about punishments that are in no way reparations in the sense of restoring a prior state of affairs, as is clearly the case with murder and other serious offenses? Perhaps punishment reestablishes order, but it cannot give back a life. These disillusioned remarks invite us to put the principal accent on the moral signification of the sanction. We need to go back to what was said above about the speech act that states the law. As was suggested in passing, the victim is publicly *recognized* as having been offended against and humiliated, that is, excluded from the regime of reciprocity owing to the fact that a crime sets up an unjust distance. This public recognition does not count for nothing. Society declares the litigant a victim in declaring the accused guilty. Yet recognition can also follow a more intimate route, one that touches *self-esteem.* Here we can say that something is restored, under names as diverse as honor, good reputation, self-respect, and, I like to emphasize the term, self-esteem—that is, the dignity attached to the moral status of the human person. Perhaps we can go a step further and suggest that this intimate recognition, touching on self-esteem, is capable of contributing to a *work of mourning* through which the wounded soul is reconciled with itself, in internalizing the figure of the lost loved object. This would be a somewhat unexpected application of the famous words of the Apostle: "the truth will set you free." In the great trials to which the disasters of our century have given rise, this work of mourning is offered not just to the victims, if they still exist, but to their descendents, kin, and allies, whose pain merits being honored. In this work of mourning, prolonging the public recognition of the offense, it is possible to recognize the moral and not just the aesthetic version of the *catharsis* offered by the tragic spectacle, according to Aristotle.

The question still has to be considered whether through the sanction something is not owed to *public opinion.* Our answer must be affirmative. Public opinion is first of all the vehicle, next the amplifier, and finally the broadcaster of the desire for vengeance. We cannot overemphasize the effect of publicity, in the sense of making public, given among others by the media to the ceremony of the trial process and the promulgation of the penalty. This publicity should consist in an education about fairness, by disciplining our impure vindictive desires. And the first threshold in this education is constituted by the *indignation,* whose name we had not yet pronounced, which, poorly distinguished from the thirst for vengeance, already begins to distance itself, once it is addressed to the dimension of injustice of the wrong that has been done. In this sense, indignation is already measured by the meaning of the law and affected by the public disturbance resulting from the infraction. Indignation, furthermore, has the virtue of binding together the emotion caused by the spectacle of the injured law and that solicited by the spectacle of the humiliated person. It is in all these senses that indignation constitutes the basic feeling starting from which public education about fairness has the chance of succeeding. In short, something is owed by the sanction to public opinion as well, which will be crowned by a certain *catharsis* of vengeance.

The last question remains: how and to what point is the sanction due to the guilty one, the condemned person? Our answer to this question conditions the whole of our proposed sequence, sanction-rehabilitation-pardon. At the beginning of our itinerary, the penal subject was implicitly taken to be passive; to be punished, to be rehabilitated, to be pardoned are all states an accused person is supposed to traverse. Yet, we said, the process had already made this person an actor, a protagonist in the hearing. How can he further become the protagonist, the actor of the sanction? Must we not say, at least in the ideal sense, that the sanction will have reached its goal, fulfilled its purpose, only if the penalty is, if not accepted, at least understood by the one who undergoes it? This limit idea—perhaps we should say, regulative idea—was implied by the idea of recognition: recognition of the litigant as victim, recognition of the accused as guilty. And if recognition pursues its trajectory into the intimacy of the person offended against in the form of a restoration of self-esteem, is not self-recognition as guilty a kind of recognition that is symmetrically expected as corresponding to this recognition on the part of the victim? I will say that we have here the regulative idea of condemnation. If sanction must have a future, under the forms we will soon speak of as rehabilitation and pardon, must it not be that, from the rendering of the sanction, the accused knows himself to be recognized at least as a reasonable, responsible being, that is, as the author of his acts? Hegel, whom I have already cited, pushes the paradox so far as to maintain that the death penalty, to which only a human being can be subjected, was a way of "honoring the guilty person as a rational being." Of course, we have better reasons to refuse the death penalty, if only the idea we have of a State that, in limiting its own impulse to vengeance, prohibits itself from itself acting like a criminal in the figure of the executioner. But at least we may retain from Hegel's argument the claim that only a reasonable being can be punished. So long as the sanction has not been recognized as reasonable by the condemned person, it has not reached this latter as a reasonable being. It is this failure of the sanction to complete its course within the framework of the trial process that opens the sequence to which we are now going to turn.

Rehabilitation

Indeed, why should we want to give a continuation to the sanction? Could we not stop there if the law, the victim, and public opinion are satisfied? The failure of the sanction to be recognized by the condemned leads us to the neighborhood of the notion of a just distance, introduced at the beginning of this meditation. Is the sanction not received, in a general way, by the condemned as an excess of distance? An excess figured, physically and geographically, by the condition of the prisoner whose incarceration marks *exclusion* from the city? And is not this excess symbolically signified by accessory penalties—loss of public and private esteem, loss of different legal and civic statuses? Whence the idea of a continuation given to the sanction as meant to reduce, degree by degree, this excess of distance and to reestablish a just distance.

In speaking of rehabilitation, the organizers of the program for this colloquy perhaps were not thinking especially of the narrowly juridical sense of rehabilitation. Even if they were right to place the accent on the sense ordinarily attached to this term, namely, the set of measures accompanying the execution of a sentence, meant to restore the condemned person to full citizenship again at the end of his sentence, it will be worthwhile to linger for a moment over the properly juridical forms of rehabilitation, particularly insofar as the idea that presides over the operations in question is that of restoring a person to the rightful place, capacity, and legal status he has lost.

There are two principal situations to consider here. First, there is the automatic and fully legal rehabilitation to which any condemned person accedes after having served his sentence and after the passing of a period proportional to the level of the infraction and the level of the case that led to the imposed sanction. The new French legal code (113/16) says about rehabilitation to one's full rights that it "wipes away all incapacities and loss of rights." We need to underscore the verb phrase "to wipe away," which is key to the continuation of our sequence that ends in pardon. This wiping away is marked by an aspect of an exception, in the sense of the solemn interruption of the sanction when it has not been applied strictly in accordance with the law. One thinks here of those grand rehabilitations of the victims of purges, constitutive of crimes of the State that happened under totalitarian regimes, where less totalitarian or more democratic regimes try to repair what has happened and to wipe out its traces to the benefit of the reestablished honor of the victims or their heirs. We can also think here of the overturning of presumed judicial errors.

Given the rarity of these situations, it is a question of quite complex procedures, having to do with the code of penal procedure and outlining the status of the one demanding rehabilitation and of its beneficiary, as well as where and how such cases are to be heard. I shall not go into these procedural questions, which add nothing to the intended end of legal rehabilitation and which we have seen expressed in such phrases as "wipe out the incapacities, reestablish the rights," that is, finally to restore a fundamental human capacity, that of the citizen as bearer of civic and legal rights.[3]

Quite clearly, it is these ideas of wiping away, of reestablishment, of restoration we refer to when we try to introduce a project of rehabilitation into the execution of a sentence. It is a question of giving the condemned person the opportunity to become a full citizen once more at the end of the sentence and therefore to end the physical and symbolic exclusion that finds its fullest expression in imprisonment.

I shall not consider here those projects of reeducation aimed at the resocialization of condemned prisoners. They stem from what we might call the pedagogy of sentencing. Instead, I shall limit myself to a few remarks that may contribute to the conceptual clarification of the term "rehabilitation," in terms consistent with the general tone of my contribution here. I propose first of all that we reflect upon the proposal, made by Antoine Garapon among others, to in-

---

3. Cf. Mireille Delmas-Marty, *Pour un droit commun* (Paris: Seuil, 1994).

troduce the concept of the continuity of public space, in order to inscribe the place of the space of the prison within, not outside the city. I want to retain just one particularly striking application of this concept which, to my knowledge at least, is still quite new. Are infractions committed in prison to be referred to the same tribunals as all other infractions committed within the space of jurisdiction of the State? Another component of reeducation to sociability: we ought to place under a single heading all those aspects of the execution of the sentence that have nothing to do with security, whether it be a question of health, work, schooling, leisure, visitation rights, even the normal expression of sexuality, and so on. The directive idea that pulls together all these many measures coming from diverse interventions is indeed still that of wiping away an incapacity, or restoring some capacity. It is in this perspective that we should take up again the discussion of the length of a sentence. If we approach this not just from the point of view of security, that is, from the point of view of the legitimate protection of society, it is the lived experience of the prisoner during the time of the sentence that has to be taken into consideration. From the few psychological studies of prisoners I have been able to examine, it seems that the time of a sentence is experienced in terms of different modalities, depending upon whether one considers the time segment closest to the trial, where time is experienced in terms of the haunting memory of this ordeal; the middle time period, where coming to terms with the prison environment is the main concern of the prisoner; or the last period of the sentence, where thoughts of liberation tend to occupy the whole of one's mental space. One result is that how these successive figures of the experience of the time of a sentence go together differs completely depending on the length of the sentence. We can assume that beyond a certain time span the execution of a sentence is equivalent to an accelerated process of desocialization. A ferocious beast, not a free person, is progressively engendered by such exclusion, at the expense of any project of reinsertion into society. This disturbing perspective even resonates with the security aspects of the execution of a sentence. I hope you will allow me to say in this regard that the notion of a "life sentence" constitutes a flagrant negation of any idea of rehabilitation, and in this sense completely negates any project of reestablishment, even in the execution of the sentence, of a just distance between the detainee and the rest of society.

Amnesty and Mercy

We cannot pass directly from the idea of rehabilitation to that of pardon without saying a word about two dispositions that we can take as intermediary between them: amnesty and mercy. We can deal quickly with the latter term, inasmuch as it consists in something like a royal privilege, having the same effects as rehabilitation as concerns wiping out principal and secondary penalties. However, we need to spend more time with amnesty, inasmuch as this sort of rehabilitation proceeds not from the juridical realm, but from the political realm, in principle the legislature, even if the leadership comes from the executive branch. If I linger over the question of amnesty, it is because, despite appearances, it in no way prepares the way to a correct understanding of the idea of pardon. In many ways, it constitutes the antithesis of pardon. Amnesty, which French republican governments have used a great deal ever since the amnesty of the Communards, in effect is a wiping away that goes well beyond the execution of sentences. To the prevention of any indictment, hence to the prevention of any pursuit of criminals, is added a prohibition even to refer to the facts themselves in terms of their criminal aspect. Therefore it is a question of a veritable institutional amnesia that invites us to act as though something never happened.[4] Several authors have observed, with some uneasiness, what there is of magic, even of desperation, in the enterprise meant to wipe out all trace of traumatic events—as if one could ever wipe away the blood from Lady Macbeth's hands! What is at issue here? Certainly, national reconciliation. And in this regard, it is perfectly legitimate to seek to mend things by forgetting the tears in the social fabric. But we may worry about the price of this reaffirmation (which I have called magical and desperate) of the indivisible character of the sovereign political body. It is for a Jacobin conception of the State which identifies its presumed rationality with universality that there is a need periodically to wipe out the traces of misdeeds done by whomever, whose memory would constitute a living denial of the claim of the State to rationality. This is a heavy price to pay. All the detrimental effects of forgetting are contained in this incredible claim to wipe

---

4. S. Gacon, "L'oubli institutionnel," *Autrement* 144 (April 1994): 98–111, in an issue entitled "Oublions nos crimes."

away the traces of public discord. It is in this sense that amnesty is the contrary of pardon, which, as I shall insist, requires memory. This is why it comes down to historians (whose task is rendered singularly difficult by this setting up of institutional forgetting) to counteract through discourse this pseudo-juridical attempt to wipe out the facts. Their task thus takes on a subversive turn, inasmuch as it leads to expressing the nemesis of the trace.

Pardon

It is difficult to situate correctly the idea of pardon on the trajectory indicated by our three terms, sanction-rehabilitation-pardon. We can say two contradictory, but perhaps equally necessary, even complementary things concerning the link between pardon and all the juridical forms that encompass sanction, rehabilitation, mercy, and amnesty. On the one hand, pardon does not belong to the juridical order. It does not stem from the same plane of the law. We could speak of it as Pascal speaks of charity in his well-known passage about the "three orders": the order of the body, the order of spirit, the order of charity. Indeed, pardon outruns the law as much through its logic as through its end. From one point of view, which we can call epistemological, it stems from an economy of the gift, in virtue of the logic of superabundance that articulates it and that has to be opposed to the logic of equivalence presiding over justice. In this regard, pardon is not just a suprajuridical but a supra-ethical value. But it nevertheless outruns the law through its end. To make sense of this, we must first say who carries it out. Absolutely speaking, this can only be the victim. In this regard, pardon is never owed. Not only cannot it not be expected, but such an expectation can be legitimately refused. To this extent, pardon must first have run into the unpardonable, that is, the infinite debt, the irreparable wrong. Having said this, although not owed, it is still not without an end. And this end has to do with memory. Its "project" is not to wipe away memory. It is not forgetting. On the contrary, its project, which is to overlook [*briser*] the debt, is incompatible with that of overlooking what is forgotten.[5] Pardon is a kind of healing of memory, the end of mourning. Delivered from the weight of debt, memory is freed for great projects. Pardon gives memory a future.

5. Olivier Abel, ed., *Le pardon. Briser la dette et l'oubli* (Paris: Ed. Autrement, 1992).

Having said this, we are not prevented from asking whether pardon may not have a kind of secondary effect on the juridical order itself, insofar as, in escaping it, pardon looms over it.

I will say two things in this regard. On the one hand, as the horizon of the sequence sanction-rehabilitation-pardon, pardon constitutes a permanent reminder that justice is the justice of human beings and that it must not set itself up as the final judgment. What is more, can we not take as the fallout of pardon on justice all the manifestations of compassion, of good will, at the very heart of the administration of justice, as though justice, touched by mercy, did not seek within its own sphere that extreme term that ever since Aristotle we have called fairness or equity. Finally, to conclude, I would like to suggest the following idea. Does it not come down to pardon to accompany justice in its effort to eradicate on the symbolic plane the sacred element of vengeance, to which I referred in passing? It is not only from savage vengeance that justice seeks to dissociate itself, but from sacred vengeance as well, in virtue of which blood calls for blood, and which itself claims the mantle of justice. On the deepest symbolic plane, what is at stake is the separation between *Dike*, the justice of humans, and *Themis*, the ultimate and shadowy refuge of the equation of Vengeance (with a capital V) and Justice (with a capital J). Does it not belong to pardon to exercise over this malicious sacred the catharsis that makes a benevolent sacred emerge from it? Greek tragedy, that of the Orestia in the first place, teaches us that the Erinyes (the avenging furies) and the Eumenides (the benevolent spirits) are one and the same. In a dazzling aside, Hegel notes in his *Principles of the Philosophy of Right:*

The Eumenides sleep, but crime awakens them.[6]

6. G. W. F. Hegel, *Philosophy of Right*, trans. T. M. Knox (New York: Oxford University Press, 1967), 247.

Conscience and the Law

The Philosophical Stakes

This essay stems from an initial refusal, my refusal to allow myself to be caught in an apparently restrictive dilemma where law, as immutable, universal, constraining, and objective, would be opposed term by term to conscience, held to be variable, circumstantial, spontaneous, and eminently subjective.

This dilemma becomes frozen in a way when, beyond this, we place it under the malicious guard of such mutually defamatory categories as dogmatism and situationalism.

The problem is not just to refute this apparent dilemma, but to construct a plausible model of correlation among the terms of a paralyzing alternative. In order to get us out of this apparent dilemma, I propose to distinguish several levels where law and conscience, in each case in a different way, can be paired up in the progressive constitution of the moral [*l'expression morale*].

I

At a first level, which we can call fundamental, I will set on the side of the pole of the law the most elementary discrimination between good and evil, and on the side of conscience the emergence of a personal identity constituted in relation to this basic discrimination. At this fundamental level, it does not make sense perhaps to speak of law in the strong sense of a moral obligation, nor of conscience in the sense of obedience to one's duty. In a sense closer to Aristotle than to Kant, I shall adopt, following my friend Charles Taylor in his *Sources of the Self*, the expression "strong evaluations," meaning by this the most stable estimations of ordinary conscience, which, through their binary structure, each express in their own way what I have called the discrimination between good and evil.[1] In this regard, ordinary moral experience has at its disposal an extraordinarily rich vocabulary that gives the pair good/bad a considerable number of variations. We need only think of such pairs of terms as honorable/ shameful, worthy/unworthy, admirable/abominable, sublime/despicable, pleasing/distressing, noble/vile, suave/abject, without forgetting what Jean Nabert had to say about the pair venerable/ unjustifiable. We have to start from this rich pallet if we are to unfold the implications of the proposed expression: strong evaluations.

The term "evaluation" expresses the fact that human life is not morally neutral, but, once it is examined, following the precept of Socrates, lends itself to a basic discrimination between what is approved as the better and what is disapproved as the worse. If the term "law" does not quite fit at this elementary level, at least in the strict sense I have spoken of, strong evaluations do present a series of characters that set us on the way to the normative sense attached to the idea of the law. Beyond the reflective labor of discrimination expressed by the variety of evaluative predicates enumerated above, we have to take into account what Taylor places under the heading of *articulation,* that is, the ordering of strong evaluations where the qualitative heterogeneity of their intended goods imposes a kind of dispersion through their intervention. To this work of coordination is added those attempts at *hierarchization* that allow us to speak, again with Taylor, of goods of a higher order, of *hypergoods.* It is to such attempts that we owe the diverse typologies of virtues and vices that occupy the place we all know in the moral treatises of ancient, medieval, and even early modern moralists of what in France we call the Classical Age. These classifications serve to mark out the median level of moral reflection, halfway from the strong evaluations considered in terms of their spontaneous dispersion and their aiming at the good life, that is, the wish for a fulfilled life, which constitutes in a way the receding horizon of such strong evaluations.

This then is what I would set at the beginning on the side of the pole of law. What will I place on the side of the pole of conscience?

---

1. Charles Taylor, *Sources of the Self: The Making of the Modern Mind* (Cambridge: Harvard University Press, 1989).

Here too I will follow the suggestion of Charles Taylor by pairing the idea of the self and that of the good. This correlation expresses the fact that the question *who?*—Who am I?—presiding over every search for personal identity, finds a first outline of an answer in the modes of adhesion by which we respond to the solicitation of strong evaluations. In this respect, we can make the different variations of the discrimination of good and evil correspond to different ways of *orienting oneself* in what Taylor calls moral space, ways of taking one's stand there in the moment and of maintaining one's place over time.

As a moral being, I am someone who assumes an orientation, takes a stand, and maintains himself in moral space. And conscience, at least at this first level, is nothing other than this orientation, this stance, and this holding on.

The analysis I am suggesting here, in a line one might call neo-Aristotelian, attests to what extent the question *what ought I to do?* is secondary in relation to the more elementary question of knowing how I might wish to live my life. Let us say, to conclude this first point, that the polarity from which the polarity of law and conscience derives can be summed up in terms of the pair "strong evaluations-strong adherence."

II

Let us pass to the second level. It is by coming to be applied to the sense of moral obligation and its negative double, interdiction, that the law accedes to the normative status ordinary usage recognizes in it. I will further draw an advantage, for the analysis I am proposing, from the fact that the term "law" comes indifferently from the register of law and that of morality. We shall see below to what point the understanding of this bond between ethics and the juridical is necessary for a correct evaluation of the role of conscience at this level. Therefore I propose that we take up the problematic of the norm beginning from the side of legality, in order to show how the movement by which legality leads back to morality is completed in the reference from morality to conscience.

Three features of what is legal will require our attention, inasmuch as they indicate the anchoring point of the dialectic of internalization of which I have already spoken.

First, *interdiction* is the stern face the law turns toward us. Even the Ten Commandments are stated in terms of this grammar of negative imperatives: you shall not kill, you shall not bear false witness, and so on. At first glance, we might be tempted to see in the interdiction only its repressive dimension, to see, if we stop with Nietzsche, only the hateful desire concealed therein. But then we would risk not taking into account what we might call the structural function of the interdiction. Lévi-Strauss has brilliantly shown this for the case of the perhaps most universally proclaimed interdiction, the incest prohibition. By forbidding men of a clan, tribe, or social group to take their mother, sister, or daughter as a sexual partner, this prohibition institutes the distinction between the bond of social alliance and the merely biological bond of reproduction. We could offer a similar demonstration as concerns the prohibition of murder, even if it were to call for a vengeful justice. By withdrawing an alleged right to vengeance from the victim, penal law sets up a just distance between two acts of violence, that of the crime and that of the punishment.[2] And it would not be difficult to offer the same demonstration for the prohibition of false testimony, which, in protecting the institution of language, helps establish the bond of mutual confidence among the members of a linguistic community.

The second feature common to the juridical and the moral norm is their claim to *universality*. I say "claim" because on the empirical plane social norms vary to a greater or lesser degree in space and time. But it is essential that in spite of this factual relativity, and through it, a validity in principle is intended. The prohibition of murder would lose its normative character if we did not hold it to apply to everyone, in every circumstance, and without exception. If, after the fact, we try to justify exceptions, whether it be a question of aid to someone in danger, say in the case of the controversial hypothesis of a just war, or, across the centuries, the death penalty, this attempt to do justice to exceptions is an homage rendered to the universality of the rule. There has to be a rule to justify the exception to the rule, a kind of rule of suspension, bearing the same requirement of legitimacy, of validity, as does the basic rule.

The third feature I want to retain concerns the connection between the norm and *human plurality*. What is forbidden, universally

---

2. Cf. the earlier chapter in this volume, "Sanction, Rehabilitation, Pardon."

condemned, are in the final analysis a whole series of wrongs done to others. A self and its other are thus the obligatory protagonists of the ethico-juridical norm. What is thereby presupposed, by law as well as by moral philosophy, is what Kant called the state of "unsociable sociability" that makes the interhuman bond so fragile.[3] In the face of this permanent threat of disorder, the most elementary requirement of the law, this same philosopher says in his "Metaphysical First Principles of the Doctrine of Right," is separating what is mine from what is yours.[4] Here we rediscover the idea of a just distance, applied this time to delimiting the competing spheres of individual liberties. Let us keep these three features in mind for the argument that follows—the structuring role of the interdiction, the claim to universal validity, the ordering of human plurality—and let us turn to the movement that, in returning toward legality from morality, finds its fulfillment in the notion of moral conscience as a counterpart to the law.

As concerns the first feature, the role of prohibition, what fundamentally distinguishes legality from morality comes to light. Legality only demands an external obedience, what Kant called mere conformity to the law, in order to distinguish respect for the law from love of duty. To this external character of legality we can add another feature that distinguishes it from morality, namely, the authorization of the use of physical force, as a way of restoring the law, of giving satisfaction to victims—in short, of allowing, as we say, the last word to the law. Insofar as mere conformity to legality is based on a fear of punishment, we understand that the passage from mere legality to veritable morality can be assimilated to a process of internalizing the norm.

As for the second feature, the claim of legality to universality, morality presents a second aspect of internalization. Opposed to the idea of an external legislator is that of a *personal autonomy,* in the strong sense of the term autonomy, interpreted by Kant as legislation that a freedom gives to itself. Through autonomy, a rational will emerges from a merely arbitrary one, by placing itself under the syn-

3. Cf. "Idea for a Universal History from a Cosmopolitan Point of View," fourth thesis, in Immanuel Kant, *On History,* trans. Lewis White Beck (Indianapolis: Bobbs-Merrill, 1963), 15–16.

4. Immanuel Kant, *The Metaphysics of Morals,* trans. Mary Gregor (New York: Cambridge University Press, 1996).

thesis of freedom and rule-governedness. However, the admiration we may have for the Kantian elegy of autonomy must not prevent us from taking into account the price we pay for this internalization of the law considered in terms of its universal angle. Only a formal rule, such as the test of universalization to which all our projects, all our life plans, in short, what Kant calls maxims of action must be submitted, can claim the kind of universality that ordinarily leaves things to mere social legality.

This formalism, it is true, finds a counterpart in the elevation to the plane of pure morality of the third feature we have recognized in legality, the role that the norm exercises as a principle of order on the plane of human plurality. It is especially among contemporary disciples of Kant, such as Rawls in his *Theory of Justice* and Habermas with his communicative ethics, that this dialogical or conversational aspect of the norm finds its fullest expression. Kant had already taken into account the plurality of moral subjects in his second formulation of the categorical imperative, requiring us to treat humanity, in our own person and in that of others, as an end in itself and not simply as a means. But it is in the idea of justice, as presented by Rawls, and of argumentation, as presented by Habermas, that we can see the dialogical or conversational implications of this second formulation of the categorical imperative fully unfolded in the figure of the mutual respect people must have for one another.

This said, it is not difficult to understand in what sense the process of internalization, through which mere social legality is raised to the level of morality, is completed in moral conscience. At this stage of our meditation, conscience is nothing other than an inward, willing obedience to the law as law, through pure respect for it and not out of mere conformity to the statement of the rule. The decisive word here is respect. In a celebrated chapter of the *Critique of Practical Reason,* Kant makes it the sole motive of the moral life.[5] This is a feeling, yes, but it is the only feeling that reason, through its authority, instills in us. Echoing Rousseau and his well-known "voice of conscience," Kant sees in this feeling both the humiliation of our avid quest for egoistic satisfactions and the exaltation of our humanity over the animal realm. But we will not be surprised to re-

5. Immanuel Kant, *Critique of Practical Reason,* trans. Lewis White Beck (Indianapolis: Bobbs-Merrill, 1956), Book I, chap. 3: "The Incentives of Pure Practical Reason," 74.

discover under the heading of the voice of conscience all the features of social legality, internalized as pure morality. The voice of conscience is first of all the voice of prohibition, as structuring, certainly, but also as rigorous. It is also the voice of the universal, which is called intransigence. Finally, under the features of the idea of justice and the goad of an ethics of discussion, the voice of conscience adds to these two aspects of rigor and intransigence that of impartiality. As impartial, the voice of conscience tells me that all other life is as important as my own, to take up the recent formulation of Thomas Nagel in his *Equality and Partiality*.[6]

This is as far as we can go with a meditation on conscience in its relation to the law, taken at its radically formal level. Three words define it: rigor, intransigence, impartiality.

The question then arises whether we can stop here. Kantian respect is certainly nothing to sneer at, above all if we develop it in terms of its dialogical applications, as in an ethics of justice or one of discussion. But are persons really recognized in their unsubstitutable singularity so long as respect is addressed more to the law than to these persons, themselves taken as the mere expression of an abstract humanity? And how are they to be so recognized, even under the sign of the idea of impartiality, if we place in parentheses those strong adhesions correlative to the strong evaluations we spoke about in the first part of this chapter, in terms of the horizon of the pursuit of a good life? My investigation of a third level of correlation between law and conscience will proceed from this question.

III

The third stage of our investigation will be devoted to what we can call moral judgment in a situation. Why make a distinct case of it? Can we not reduce this stage to the simple idea of an application of a general norm to a particular case? Beyond the fact that moral judgment in a situation does not reduce to the simple idea of application, as we shall see, this latter idea itself is far from reducing to the overly simple idea one too often makes of it. To apply a norm to a particular case is an extraordinarily complex operation that implies a style of

6. Thomas Nagel, *Equality and Partiality* (New York: Oxford University Press, 1991).

interpretation irreducible to the mechanism of the practical syllogism. Here again, law constitutes a good introduction to the dialectic of moral judgment in a situation. The complex process at the end of which a case is placed under a norm involves two interwoven processes of interpretation.[7] On the one side, that of the case considered, the problem is to reconstitute a plausible, a reasonable history, the history or rather the interweaving of histories constitutive of what we call a case, or better an "affair." The hearing, as the centerpiece of the trial, reveals how difficult it is to disentangle a univocally true narrative from the confrontation between the rival versions proposed by the parties involved in litigation. The difficulty is no less on the side of the norm. It is not always immediately clear that this case should be placed beneath this norm. What is called the qualification of a litigious act results from a work of interpretation applied to the norm itself. Recent affairs in France, such as that of HIV-contaminated blood being given to hemophiliacs, remain controversial as concerns the apparently simple decision of indicating within the judicial *corpus* the norm that should be applied in such a case. Their application therefore lies at the crossroads of a double chain of interpretation, with the facts on one side and the rule on the other. A judgment in situation thus comes about at the point of intersection of these two lines of interpretation. We can say that argumentation and interpretation are inseparable, the argumentation constituting the logical framework and the interpretation the inventive framework of the process ending in the making of a decision.

What are we to say then about the relation between law and conscience? It would be an error to think that the idea of law has disappeared from the judgment in situation. In fact, it is a question of saying what the law is in a determined circumstance. In this regard, the pronounced sentence would not have any juridical meaning if it were not deemed fair, equitable, in the sense that Aristotle gives the term "equity" when the norm covers a singularity equal to that of the case considered. As for conscience, it is nothing other than the inner, heartfelt conviction that inhabits the soul of the judge or the jury, equitably pronouncing the judgment. In this regard, we can say that the equity of a judgment is the objective face for which this inner conviction constitutes the subjective guarantor. The tie between in-

7. Cf. the earlier chapter "Interpretation and/or Argumentation."

ner conviction and the speech act consisting in stating the law in a particular circumstance removes the judgment in situation from pure arbitrariness.

But we have so far considered just one category of moral judgments in a situation, the one we can place under the heading of application. There are many other occasions for exercising moral judgment in a situation. Application assumes the existence of a *corpus* of relatively homogeneous laws that have not been called into question, at least at the time of the trial. But there exist a number of more embarrassing situations where it is the very reference to the law that causes a problem. We must first consider the case where several norms clash, as we see in Greek tragedy, for instance when Antigone and Creon both figure as respectable spiritual values, but in terms of a narrow perspective that makes them incompatible, to the point of bringing about the deaths of the antagonists. This tragic dimension of action calls for what Sophocles calls *to phronein*, the act of "judging wisely." It is the virtue Aristotle would raise to a higher rank under the name *phronesis*, a term translated into Latin as *prudentia*, which we can translate as practical wisdom or, still better, as wisdom in judgment. The first part of this chapter prepared us for this confrontation with such modes of the tragic dimension of action, starting with strong evaluations relating to heterogeneous and sometimes competing goods. It is this tragic dimension of action that is left out in a wholly formal conception of moral obligation, reduced to the test of universalization of a maxim. It is largely overlooked too in the Rawlsian conception of justice, where the confrontation between substantial goods is set aside to the benefit of a wholly formal procedural rule. It is no less overlooked in an ethics of discussion that also places itself in a perspective where convictions are reduced to conventions the protagonists in the discussion are assumed to have surpassed in assuming what is called a post-conventional posture. It is the task of any formalism, in eliminating all reference to the good life, to elude those situations of conflict linked to the evaluation of goods situated along the trajectory of the wish for a good life.

But the tragedy that has been pushed out the door comes in again through the window once the irreducible diversity of basic social goods is taken into consideration, as a comprehensive theory of justice must do. We are then confronted with what in a revision of his theory of justice Rawls himself calls "reasonable disagreements." I like this expression that nicely captures the virtue of prudence. The fragmentation of political ideals, of spheres of justice, and, even in the juridical domain, the multiplication of sources of law and the blossoming of codes of jurisdiction invites us to take seriously this idea of a reasonable disagreement.

But things become more serious when it is no longer just norms that enter into conflict—once the respect owed to the universal norm confronts the respect owed to singular persons. It is indeed a question of the tragic dimension of action when the norm remains recognized as a party in the debate, in the conflict that opposes it to solicitude for human poverty and suffering. Wisdom in judging consists in elaborating fragile compromises where it is a matter less of deciding between good and evil, between black and white, than between gray and gray, or, in the highly tragic case, between bad and worse.

Is conscience then reduced to arbitrariness, as some situational ethicists suggest? No. As above, with the judge charged with stating the law in a singular situation, the ethicist, faced with the tragic dimension of action, states the better or the less bad, as it appears at the end of a debate where norms weigh no less than do persons. In this sense, his inner conviction has as its objective correlate the *apparent better* thing to do in the circumstance. What is more, if this apparent better, to conserve the vocabulary forged on the occasion of the juridical judgment in situation, issues from an intersecting play of argumentation and interpretation, the decision taken at the end of a debate with oneself, at the heart of what we may call our innermost forum, our heart of hearts, will be all the more worthy of being called *wise* if it issues from a council, on the model of our French national consultative council on ethics, or on the model of the small circle bringing together relatives, doctors, psychologists, and religious leaders at the bed of someone who is dying. Wisdom in judging and the pronouncement of wise judgment must always involve more than one person. Then conscience truly merits the name *conviction*. Conviction is the new name that the strong adhesion of our first analysis now receives, after having traversed the rigor, intransigence, and impartiality of abstract ethics, and having confronted the tragic dimension of action.

S O U R C E S   O F   O R I G I N A L   P U B L I C A T I O N

"Le concept de responsabilité. Essai d'analyse sémantique." Presentation before l'Institut des hautes études sur la justice (IHEJ). *Esprit* (November 1994).

"Après *Théorie de la justice* de John Rawls." In F. Châtelet, O. Duhamel, and E. Pisier, eds., *Dictionnaire des oeuvres politiques.* Paris: Presses Universitaires de France, 1995.

"La pluralité des instances de justice." Presentation before the Institut des hautes études sur la justice.

"Jugement esthétique et jugement politique selon Hannah Arendt." *Revue semestrielle d'anthropologie et d'histoire* (1994).

"Interprétation et/ou argumentation." Revised version of a presentation to the colloquy "What is Justice?" held 6–10 December 1993, University of Dresden.

"L'acte de juger." Presentation before l'Institut des hautes études sur la justice. *Esprit* (July 1992).

"Sanction, réhabilitation, pardon." Presentation to a colloquy on "Conscience in Contemporary Society," organized by *La Croix, l'Evenement,* held 30 April 1994. In *Justice ou vengeance.* Paris: Editions du Centurion, 1994.

"La conscience et la loi. Enjeux philosophiques." Presentation to a colloquy titled "Conscience in Contemporary Society" organized by the Avocats au barreau de Paris, held at the Cathedral School in June 1994.

I NDEX